HATTIE'S FAMILY
Through the Eyes of a Dairymaid

KB Taylor

www.kb-taylor.com

BOOT TOP BOOKS
Lacey, WA

Hattie's Family is a work of fiction. All names, characters, places and incidents, either are the creation of the author's imagination or used fictitiously. Any resemblance to actual persons, living or dead, businesses, companies, events or locales is entirely coincidental.

Copyright© 2020 by Karen Bishop - All Rights Reserved. No part of this publication may be reproduced, stored, or transmitted in any form without the prior written permission of the publisher, except brief excerpts for printed reviews/articles.

Library of Congress Cataloging-in-Publication Data
Author: Bishop, Karen (KB Taylor)
Story collaboration, historical research, and the
Sonnet pg: 247, Taylor, Diane
LCCN: 2020947415
Hattie's Family/KB Taylor-1ˢᵗ ed.
p. cm: includes bibliographical references.
Hattie travels across country from her Wisconsin farm to Washington State to tend to her young nieces and assist in a high-end mercantile. Not an easy task for a girl who stutters.
ISBN: 9781733369725 (Print) 9781733369732 (ebook)
1. Historical Mercantile—fiction. 2. Historical Family—fiction 3. Pacific Northwest (Washington State) 19th century—fiction. 4. Sisters—Fiction. 5. Stammering—fiction 6. Magic Healer—fiction 7. Logging Camps—fiction
Printed in the United States of America
December 2020
Boot Top Books, Lacey, WA

Figure 1

**(Courtesy of Taylor Family Collection)
(Note: the giant "V" sign in front of the Veysey Store)**

VEYSEY STORE
(Veysey pronounced Vee-cee)

The Veysey Bros. Stores were in operation in Grays Harbor County for THIRTY-FIVE YEARS (1892-1927) There were six stores: one in Hoquiam, one in Elma, one in Aberdeen, and three in Montesano.

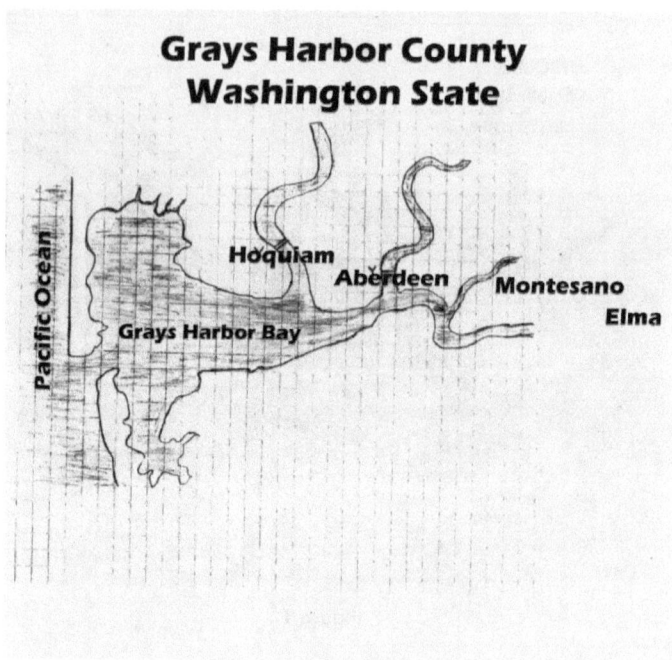

Figure 2

HATTIE'S FAMILY
Through the eyes of a dairymaid

KB Taylor

CHAPTER ONE
HOQUIAM, WASHINGTON

> **WESTERN UNION TELEGRAM**
>
> Received at: Transmitted from: Chehalis, WA
> Waupaca, WI   08/01/1903   11:00 a.m.
>
> Mother. NEED HELP. Ticket on hold at train station.
>
> Not recovered from back surgery.
> Hospital quarantined. Smallpox breakout.
> One hundred miles from home.
> Need help with our girls and our store. Please come.
>
> Your son - Leon

"GET PACKED," Mother told Hattie, handing her the telegram. "You're heading west to Washington."

Hattie bit her lip. She had never been farther than sixty miles from their Wisconsin dairy farm. "But Mother, my st-st-stuttering."

"You'll do fine, Hattie. You're going."

AT THE HOQUIAM TRAIN STATION, Hattie set her carpetbag atop her trunk, then dragged the trunk closer to the street, stopping to sit on it until she finally reached the road. Sitting on the trunk again, she looked at the distant hilltops before her, one after another dense with trees. Wisconsin had forest too, but none as never-ending as these appeared to be. She turned her head toward the bay. In the distance, sawmills buzzed and a tugboat blared its deep-throated horn, towing a tall-mast ship up the channel.

She checked the street again and wondered if she'd been forgotten or worse, not expected at all. *What if they didn't receive Mother's telegram? Why did I let her convince me to come? I don't belong here. I'm a dairymaid. I know nothing about working in a mercantile. And how do I control my stuttering?*

The journey to Hoquiam had been a long one and Hattie had barely gotten any rest on the train, but she was used to a lack of sleep from all the required work on the dairy farm. Always up before dawn to milk the cows, but it didn't start with sitting on the milking stool. First, she had to prepare the cow and the stall, which included tossing cow manure and cleaning the cow's udder and butt. Thinking about her farm life brought more worry to her fitting in.

At the sight of a wagon, she craned her neck, and caught the eye of a handsome young man. With a quick nod, he tipped the brim of his hat. Hattie quickly looked away, but was very aware of his presence when he stopped his wagon a few feet from where she was sitting.

Who is that? Ivar thought. Not hesitating to find out, he jumped off his wagon and walked directly to her.

"Pardon me, miss. Do you need help?"

"No, I'm w-w-waiting for a ride."

He scanned the empty station and refocused on her again. "Appears you've been here awhile."

When their eyes met again and he broadened his smile, Hattie's heart flittered. "Yes, I have been."

"Let me pick up my load, then let's see how I might help you."

After he steadied a small wooden crate into his buckboard, he removed his brown-felt hat, threw it into the back of the wagon, and raked his hand through his thick blond hair.

Oh my, he's handsome. Hattie felt an ambush of heat to her cheeks as he neared.

"Where are you headed?" he asked.

"Vee-cee Store." Keeping her sentences short and stretching out her words minimized her stuttering. She had learned that at an early age.

"I'm going that way. I can drop you off."

Hattie looked up the street again, and then nodded. "Yes, I'd be obliged."

"My name is Ivar Ekola," he told her as he hoisted her trunk into his wagon.

"I'm H-H-Hattie." She shook her head from the frustration of her stuttering.

"Nice to meet you, Hattie. Why the Veysey Store?"

She sighed louder than she intended. "M-m-my last name is Vee-cee."

He studied her face. "I see the Veysey family resemblance, especially to Josie."

Hattie had only seen young pictures of her niece, Josie, but had no desire to contradict his assessment. She cleared her throat. "Ekola, I have not heard that n-n-name before."

"Finnish," he said. "A lot of Scandinavians settled here. Most work in the logging camps and some at the mills." He pointed to the right. "That section's called Finn Town, but I'd advise you to only visit by day. Gets a bit rough-neck at night. Look," he said, motioning to the street. "Your ride."

Hattie glanced at the wagon pulling up. It reminded her of the peddler ones back home. On this one, the tall wooden sideboards had signage painted in coal black that advertised:

VEYSEY MERCANTILE—LADIES, CHILDREN, AND GENTS

The driver was a stocky girl with chestnut-brown pigtails, a freckled face, and dressed in a plaid shirt and bib overalls. She slid down off the wagon just as Ivar reached her. While the two talked, he pointed to Hattie.

The girl gasped and looked, then rushed over. "Aunt Harriet," she said. "Is that you?"

Harriet was Hattie's proper name, but rarely used it. Hattie nodded. "Call me H-H-Hattie."

"I'm Mabs," the young girl said, hugging her. She stepped back. "Where's Grandma?"

"N-n-not coming." Hattie paused. "Mabs? I don't recall that...name."

"Mabel," she corrected. "I'm sorry about not being at the station, but Mr. Connell's cow invention caught my eye and I had to stop. But I have been checking the train daily." Mabs looked at Hattie quizzically. "I never knew you stuttered."

Trying to hide the redness burning her cheeks, she looked at the ground. "Worse when I g-g-get nervous."

"We all get spiked with nerves," said Mabs. "I turn green as a cucumber talking in front of my class."

Hattie smiled at her niece. She instantly liked Mabs and found her friendly, outgoing, and no hesitation to speak her mind—all traits Hattie wished that she possessed.

Ivar interjected with a chuckle. "What was Mr. Connell doing this time?"

"He had a harness on the butt of a tan and white cow," said Mabs. "His sign said cow hopple."

"Did the c-c-cow have diamond-shaped patches?" asked Hattie. Mabs nodded. "Bet it was a J-J-Jersey."

Ivar arched his eyebrow. "Sounds like you know your cows."

"I was r-r-raised on...a dairy farm." Stretching her sentences again to minimize her stuttering. "Jerseys can be kickers and...t-t-tail smackers," said Hattie. "Hopples help."

"It didn't appear to be working too good," Mabs added. "Guess we better get going."

Hattie followed Mabs over to her wagon, and just as she readied herself to step up, Ivar clutched onto her arm. She glanced back at him with a bashful smile.

"It was awful nice meeting you, Hattie. I'll deliver your trunk within the hour." He tapped the wagon, turned around, and walked away.

"Josie will be in high-spirits to hear that," Mabs quipped. "She's love sick for Ivar, but he's now a college man and has outgrown her ways. But she's got every other boy in town at her feet and puts-on like the Queen of Sheba."

CHAPTER TWO

TRAVELING DOWN EIGHTH Street the wagon wheels clicked and clacked on the planked streets. Hattie observed that almost every building was from lumber and so were the roads and walkways.

"Your town's b-b-bigger than I thought," she said, reading the storefront signage as they passed: druggist, eateries, haberdashery, sundries, to name a few.

"Hoquiam's booming from all the lumber mills," said Mabs. "Schooners arrive weekly, most are from San Francisco. And lots of stores. Ours is the best in town."

Hattie grinned. "So many r-r-roads are planked."

"Covers the mud and sloughs from all the rain. That's why everything's so green. Whoa," said Mabs, pulling on the reins. "We're here."

She stopped the wagon in front of a very tall *V*-shaped sign. The word CLOTHING was painted vertically on one side of the giant *V*, the other side advertised BOOTS and SHOES. A board across the top spelled out VEYSEY, the store name.

Pretty clever sign, Hattie thought, sliding down off the wagon. She walked over to two oversized front windows. Inside the large displays were life-size mannequins in pink and white-ruffled dresses, ostrich-feather hats, and on the floor, fringe-beaded handbags, lacy parasols, and button-up boots.

Hattie followed Mabs through two massive double-glassed doors and into the mercantile. "Goodness,"

Hattie said, shaking her head as she placed her carpetbag down and scanned the store.

The store was one of the largest that she had ever seen: planked floors that seemed to go on forever and shelving all organized with notions, ribbons, fabric, and so many other things that extended half way up the walls toward tall ceramic ceilings. A special corner was sectioned off for dresses, hats, and boots.

"What a f-f-fine store."

"That's what I told you. I'll get my sisters."

Hattie watched her niece's approach. The tallest had to be Josephine, next was Evelyn, and lastly, Matilda, pint-size, round face, and dark hair styled in a Dutch-boy straight-cut.

"Aunt Hattie," Mabs said. "I told them you stuttered, so no reason for you to be nervous, and we all go by nicknames." She pointed to each sister. "Josephine is Josie, and Evelyn goes by Eva, and Matilda, Tillie."

Tillie wrapped her tiny arms around Hattie's thighs. Eva bashfully followed her younger sister, but stood back.

"Happy to meet you, Tillie." Hattie said, stroking the young girl's hair, "and Eva, how...do you do?"

Eva, with almond-colored braids, an oval face, and blue eyes, grinned wide, exposing a missing side-tooth.

"How...old are you... g-g-girls...now?"

Mabs spoke up. "Eva's ten, Tillie's seven, I'm fifteen, and Josie just turned eighteen."

"I'll speak for myself, thank you," Josie huffed.

Josie had a similar five-foot-six height to Hattie, thin build, and oval face, and they both had long wavy hair, except Josie's was butterscotch-brown. But Josie had no plainness to her. She had pouty lips, soft-blushed cheeks, and lush lashes that drew a person to her porcelain-doll face.

"What a b-b-beautiful dress, Jo...see."

"Nothing special," she said, brushing down a crease in her pink ruffled skirt. Josie folded her arms and stared at Hattie. "How old are you?"

Trying to conceal her stuttering again, Hattie talked in long pauses. "I turn...twenty in...another several w-w-weeks."

"So, you're out of school. I don't recall a letter telling us you graduated."

"S-s-school only went through the eighth grade. I was h-h-home schooled after that."

"Oh," Josie said in a snobbish tone. "This fall will be my final year of high school, then on to the university."

"V-v-very good."

"Good, indeed," she said, flashing her piercing green eyes at Hattie. "I'm the top of my class. And since it appears that I'm better educated, there is no reason for you to work in the mercantile."

Even though Hattie didn't relish the idea of helping in the store, she had come to help. "Your father sent a telegram r-r-requesting..."

"He didn't ask for you," said Josie. "He wanted Grandma." She wanted to add *not some farm girl with an eighth-grade education*, but she restrained.

"Mother t-t-taught me bookkeeping. She was a school teacher...you know."

"You'll not be my boss and Mr. and Mrs. Bailey manage the mercantile just fine. Maybe you can go to Aberdeen and help in Uncle Charles' store."

Aberdeen was the neighboring town and Charles was Hattie's oldest brother.

"Stop it, Josie," Mabs said. "You know that Uncle Charles is on his honeymoon." She turned to Hattie. "He should be back early next month. I'll take you over to see him then."

"That would be nice," said Hattie.

"If you must work in our store, stay in the back and let Mrs. Bailey and me handle the sales," Josie added. When a tiny bell signaled a customer had come in, Josie waltzed toward the woman. "Bonjour, Mrs. Tuttle."

Hattie smiled at her nieces who stood frozen, glancing at one another, too embarrassed to speak.

"We're sorry, Aunt Hattie," Mabs said. "Josie's gotten used to being in charge. She can be nice as long as she's not challenged. She's been trying to stop me from making deliveries, but I've ignored her."

"Who w-w-would do it, if you…didn't?"

"No one. Mrs. Cushman convinced Josie that delivery was an unnecessary courtesy, but I reminded Josie that Father said all customers are good business."

"Who's Mrs. Cushman?"

"One of our best customers," Mabs said. "She's married to one of the richest lumber barons on the harbor. She's teaching Josie proper etiquette, and if you ask me, it hasn't been too positive."

"Do your p-p-parents know about her influence?"

"Yes. When Mrs. Cushman asked if she could take Josie under her wing, Mother considered it an honor, but she wouldn't be happy with the way Josie talked to you."

"I'm sure...things...will iron out," said Hattie, but truthfully, she wasn't so sure. "I'd like to get settled in, may we g-g-go to your home now?"

Tillie reached for her aunt's hand. "I'll show you," pulling Hattie to a stairway. Her tiny finger directed upward. "Up there."

"You live above the store?" Tillie nodded. Hattie had assumed that they had a house nearby. Is that a fact her brother forgot to mention to their mother?

Entering the living quarters, Hattie gaped again. The sitting room was as elegant as any she had ever seen: tall mahogany-framed windows overlooked Eighth Street, the main street in town, and on the opposite wall, was a brick fireplace with a silver-framed mirror above and a taupe velvet sofa facing the hearth.

Tillie pulled Hattie along as the others followed. "This is Mama's kitchen."

"Nice," said Hattie. The tour continued down a long hallway.

"Our bedrooms," Mabs said, motioning to two doors on the same side. "Tillie and Eva share this room and Josie and I sleep next door." She pointed to another door at the end of the hall. "That's the water closet to wash up and use the privy."

Hattie nodded as if she understood, but she really didn't. On the dairy farm, they had an outhouse and a well and hauled water into the house.

Mabs opened a door across from the girl's bedrooms. "This is Mother and Father's quarters. You'll sleep here."

Hattie found the bedroom to be as lavish as the sitting room. She felt like an intruder. "I shouldn't sleep in here. Let me t-t-trade with one of you."

"No," said Mabs. "Mother sent a telegram and instructed for Grandma to have this room. I know she'd want the same for you."

Hattie set her carpetbag on the floor, but she had a sinking feeling that Josie might not agree, and if Hattie had to wager odds, she predicted she'd be moved by nightfall. And she was right. By bedtime, Hattie's carpetbag had been relocated to Mabs' room and Josie had settled into her parents' quarters and locked the door.

HOQUIAM VEYSEY STORE - 1900

Figure 3
(Courtesy of University of Washington Libraries,
Special Collections, WAS 1206)

Note: Giant "V" Sign in the front of the store

Figure 4 - ECONOMY STORE – 1900
(Courtesy of the Taylor Family Collection)

HOQUIAM VEYSEY STORE–1900

Figure 5
(Courtesy of University of Washington Libraries, Special Collections, WAS 1207)

CHAPTER THREE

HATTIE STUDIED HERSELF in the mirror, ensuring no loose wisps in her hair. When she had met the Baileys the other day, she overheard Mrs. Bailey comment to Josie how untidy and plain that Hattie looked, but Mrs. Bailey had no room to talk. In addition to her noisy shoes and dark attire, Mrs. Bailey was skinny as a fence rail, had a pointy nose, long face, and round chin, plus a hot and cold temperament that could regulate a room faster than a fire. The only trait she shared with her jokester husband was her brown, gray-streaked hair that she wore in a taut bun. His brown hair was balding.

On the final step down into the store, Hattie took a deep breath and walked to the front counter. No matter how much Hattie practiced, she couldn't control her stuttering around this rigid woman and it twisted her stomach into knots. "G-g-good morning."

Mrs. Bailey puckered her lips and scrutinized Hattie up and down. She circled to Hattie's back. "Acceptable," is all she said. "Come along."

Walking Hattie through the store, Mrs. Bailey straightened racks as they passed. "Restock, tidy, and dust," she told Hattie. "And keep the stockroom in good order." She pointed to a shelf. "Needs more socks."

"Okay," said Hattie, hurrying off to the stockroom. When she pulled back the curtain, she found Mr. Bailey asleep in an old padded chair.

He squinted and sat up. "Just needed a bit of a rest," he chuckled. "Don't tell the missus."

Hattie gave him a quick nod and gathered an armful of socks. While restocking the shelf, she heard the clip clop of Mrs. Bailey's sharp-toed shoes coming toward her.

"Have you seen Mr. Bailey?"

Hattie froze. She cleared her throat. "Uh...uh."

"Never mind, I'll find him myself. Wilber ...Wilber."

He ambled out of the back room with a sly-as-a-fox smirk on his face. "Yes, dear."

She huffed. "Did you ever get those felt hats down?"

"It slipped my mind. I've been awfully busy." He walked over to the ladder in front of the tall shelves and slid it along the top rail. "I'll fetch them now."

Hattie questioned if such a portly man should be up on the ladder, but he climbed up. Descending with the hats piled atop his head, he removed them with a grin and a bow, and handed them to his wife.

"You rascal," she said, her voice softening.

He pecked her cheek. "Off to have a smoke."

Looking at her husband, Mrs. Bailey's eyes twinkled, but when she caught Hattie's glance, she creased her brow and stomped toward her. "Plain girls shouldn't wear such drab attire. What other color dresses do you have?"

"B-b-blue, but that's for church. My other...one is b-b-brown, but a darker shade than this...one."

"That won't do," the older woman snorted. She studied Hattie then walked over to the rack, grabbing a light-green gingham dress and handing it to her. "This should fit. I'll mark it as an I.O.U. on the ledger."

"I-I-I don't have m-m-money for this."

"You're a Veysey. Can't have you looking like a vagrant. You can work it off."

Hattie reluctantly carried the dress to the changing room. Viewing herself in the mirror, she was surprised how much nicer she looked and how well it fit. Even though she found Mrs. Bailey abrupt, she had to admit that the older woman knew her trade. Hattie shyly pulled back the curtain and stepped out.

Mrs. Bailey circled around her, tugging on the skirt. "Much better," she said in an approving tone.

"Th-th..."

"Thank you. Is that what you're trying to say?"

Hattie felt her face redden as she nodded, but it was not the first time Mrs. Bailey had finished Hattie's words and more than likely not the last.

"You can update the window display." She handed Hattie two yellow and blue ruffled dresses, of different styles, and then escorted her to the window.

The window display faced the street. Once inside it, Hattie felt like she was in a fishbowl and prayed that no one would stop to watch. After she started dressing the mannequins, she found it enjoyable and forgot about the outside world. She stepped back and examined her work. *Something's lacking. It should draw the eye.* She climbed out of the window and hurried to the ribbons, buttons, and bows, selecting different hues of blues and yellows. Back inside the display adding her touches, she didn't notice that a customer had walked in until she heard Mrs. Bailey's foghorn voice. "Hello, Mrs. Ekola."

Ivar's mother?

Hattie peeked out the curtain that shielded the window display from the store and studied the statuesque woman. The fur collar on her navy wool coat brushed against her face, highlighting rosy cheeks and silky flaxen hair braided into a bun.

"Ivar and Josie are on their way," the blonde woman said. "He needs a new suit."

"We have plenty for him to choose from," said Mrs. Bailey. "He's such a handsome boy."

"Yes," said Mrs. Ekola in a prideful tone. "He and Josie are the perfect pair. Josie mentioned an aunt. I'd like to invite her to tea."

"Oh, no," Mrs. Bailey said, lowering her voice but not soft enough to conceal from Hattie's ears. "She's a country girl. Not the type you'd want to entertain."

"Not sure what you mean?" Mrs. Ekola replied.

"She stammers. It's mortifying to have her in the store, never knowing when a customer might ask her to talk. I assure you, you'd be quite frustrated."

"I see," said Mrs. Ekola with a sympathetic tone. "How awful for the girl."

"I do what I can to keep her shielded, but..."

"You're a kind woman," Mrs. Ekola added.

Hattie sighed and slumped to the floor. *How dare Mrs. Bailey talk about me like that.* Much as she wanted to shrug it off, she couldn't. "Stop it," she muttered, scolding herself. When she heard tapping on the window, she jolted her head up and saw Josie and Ivar staring at her. She quickly turned away, stood, and stepped out of the window display. Mrs. Bailey and Mrs. Ekola had their backs to her, conversing, which allowed Hattie to hurry past and toward the stairs, but then the door opened and Josie called out.

"Aunt Hattie, wait."

Hattie slowly turned around. Her stomach tightened when all eyes focused on her.

Josie strode toward her with a steady pace. "You *must* meet Mrs. Ekola. Ivar told her we could be twins. I wanted her to see for herself how absurd that was." Before Hattie could respond, Ivar walked up wearing a beige tweed suit. With his blond hair slicked down and parted to one side, he looked more like a banker than the carefree young man who had offered her a ride.

"Hi, Hattie," Ivar said. "Good to see you."

"H-h-hello...Ivar."

Mrs. Bailey, in her noisy shoes, clip-clopped toward them. Mrs. Ekola was at her side. "Doesn't Hattie look nice in her new dress?" Mrs. Bailey remarked.

Hattie blushed.

"Isn't that the dress I had my eye on?" Josie said.

"Yes," Mrs. Bailey responded, "but she needed something decent to wear in the store." Hattie stood motionless, wishing she could disappear. Mrs. Bailey continued. "Besides it's far too simple a dress for you."

Josie huffed, and when she glanced at Mrs. Ekola and Ivar, who were giving her a disapproving stare, she changed her demeanor. "I'm sorry, Aunt Hattie. How very selfish of me. The dress is better suited for you."

Even though Josie tried to sound sincere, Hattie detected a dishonest sweetness in her tone.

Ivar's mother stepped forward. "I'm Mrs. Ekola."

"N-n-nice to meet you. I'm H-H-Hattie."

Mrs. Ekola patted Hattie's hand. "Pleasure's mine."

Hattie hesitated awkwardly before looking away. Relief washed through her when Ivar spoke up.

"Who's going to help me pick out a suit?"

Josie latched onto his arm. "Me, of course." She glanced at Hattie. "Don't set a plate for me tonight. I'm dining with the Ekolas."

"Okay," said Hattie. "I b-b-best get started on supper for the girls." She nodded to Mrs. Ekola, and then turned back to the stairs, chastising herself with every step up. *Why can't I just once not stutter?*

The tall ceramic ceilings magnified voices. "I can't imagine being stricken with such a curse," Hattie heard Mrs. Ekola say. "Thankfully, it wasn't passed onto Josie."

"Indeed," Mrs. Bailey replied.

Hattie quickly opened and closed the door behind her. Leaning against it, she folded her hands into a prayer. "Dear Lord, please give me strength and courage." Her stomach gnawed from the humiliation and tears welled in her eyes. *How can I ever face Mrs. Ekola again?*

CHAPTER FOUR

A PANIC KNOCK startled Hattie. She opened the front door and saw Mrs. Bailey's stricken face. "Please c-c-come in," Hattie said, stepping aside.

"I didn't come to visit," she blurted. "Mr. Bailey has dropsy. The doctor said it could affect his heart."

"Th-th-that's terrible."

"You'll have to run the store."

Hattie had worked the week with Mrs. Bailey, but most of her time was spent in the stockroom or dusting the shelves, not assisting customers.

Hattie's eyes widened. "W-w-what?"

The woman scowled at Hattie. "There'll be none of that stuttering. Josie thinks you do it for attention. I'm wondering if she might be right. On purpose or not, you must control it. It's an embarrassment to the store."

Hattie bit her lip and nodded. She had noticed Mrs. Bailey's closeness to Josie, but it stabbed at Hattie's heart to know that Josie would gossip with such spitefulness.

"Mrs. B-B-Bailey, I don't know how to r-r-run the store on my own."

"Help the customers, simple as that, and track the sales. The ledger and keys are under a mat on the front counter. The money box is in the cage." She bore her eyes through Hattie. "You do know how to add and subtract, don't you?"

Insulted by Mrs. Bailey's question, Hattie responded with a curt, "Yes."

"Hope you're telling me the truth." She didn't wait for Hattie's response. "Remember, record every sale and try to make proper change. If you get stuck, Josie can instruct you. Not sure when I'll be returning." Without another word, Mrs. Bailey turned around and hurried down the stairs.

STANDING AT THE STORE COUNTER, jitters pulsed through her. *You can do this*, repeated in Hattie's head, but then fear crept in about her stuttering. A good day meant that her stuttering wasn't so dreadful, but an unmanageable repeated stumble could paralyze her emotionally for days. She prayed that today wouldn't become a bad one.

Scanning the store, she spotted only a handful of hankies on display and raced to the stockroom to get more, but the bin was empty. A piece of paper inside stated a *reorder has been placed, expected next week.*

She grabbed several styles of men's socks and spread them out on the hankie counter, but they looked out of place. Then she remembered the hankies she had made for the girls. They were still in her traveling trunk, which had been stored under the staircase. She darted to it, pulled out the packet wrapped in twine, and removed twelve embroidered hankies.

Arranging them under the store ones, she noted how nice hers blended. *No one should notice. These will be good fillers until the real ones arrive.* When the clock bonged nine times, Hattie squared her shoulders, marched over to the massive front doors, and unlocked them. No sooner had she reached the front counter again, the door pushed open, the tiny bell above dinged, and two women walked in. Both customers were outfitted in swooping A-shaped dresses with braided bodices.

The younger of the two smiled at Hattie. "You must be the aunt?" Hattie nodded. "I'm Mrs. Cushman, Josie's etiquette instructor." Mrs. Cushman had raven hair, sparkling blue eyes, and an hourglass figure complemented by her peacock-blue attire.

"This is Mrs. Wiggins," said Mrs. Cushman.

"Hello," said Hattie, responding with a quick nod to the plump woman.

Mrs. Wiggins, with her straw-colored locks, insipid face, and overly large nose, was wearing a wheat-colored dress that washed out her complexion.

Mrs. Cushman pulled off her black leather gloves and craned her neck side to side, looking about the store. "Where's Mrs. Bailey?"

Hattie took a deep breath, praying her next words wouldn't be a stutter, but knowing full well that they would. "Mr. B-B-Bailey...has t-t-taken...ill."

She and Mrs. Wiggins stared at Hattie as if Hattie had grown a wart on her nose, and then they glanced at one another with raised eyebrows. Mrs. Cushman finally spoke. "Give Mrs. Bailey our best," she said, pulling her gloves back on. "Come, Ann. Don't want to miss the streetcar."

Whispering as they walked out, Hattie heard one of them say, "What an odd girl. Is it possibly a mental disorder?"

Hattie puffed out a sigh and stared up at the ceiling. *What was I thinking? I can't do this.* When she heard the door open again, panic washed through her as she watched two nicely dressed women walk in and head over to the accessory shelves. Talking to one another and paying no attention to Hattie at all, the women approached the counter. The one holding four handkerchiefs dropped them on the glass and reached for her handbag. Hattie gasped when she saw that they were *her* hankies, not the store ones. "How much?" the women asked.

Panic pulsed through Hattie again. She had never intended for anyone to buy her hankies, but she wasn't going to attempt to explain it either. She thought for a moment, recalling the store ones sold for twenty-five cents each, so she lowered the price.

"Half...dollar," she said slowly, without a stutter.

"For all four?" the woman questioned.

"Y-y-yes."

The woman paid and walked out with her friend.

Still shaken from her earlier encounter with Mrs. Cushman and now with someone buying her hankies, Hattie doubted if her nerves could last such an active day. She walked over to the dress rack and looked at all the lovely styles, feeling the different fabrics: taffetas and satins, to name just two. Those were on the fancy racks. The simpler dresses of gingham and printed cottons were at the back and more suited to her, but secretly she wished she could wear another style, just once. But then her mother's words popped into her head. "What foolishness, Hattie. You're a farm girl. You have no need for that."

What really had caught Hattie's eye were the new day skirts: slim at the hips, pleated at the front, and full below the knees, usually worn with a white or ivory drop-waist blouse. Soon as the skirts had arrived from San Francisco, they flew off the racks, mostly bought by younger women in their twenties. Hattie guessed that Josie would be sporting this fashion when she went off to college next year.

The ding of the doorbell announced another customer. No matter how Hattie tried to calm her nerves, every time someone entered the store, her stomach shook like jelly. She pasted on a smile and turned, ready to do her best and praying she wouldn't stutter. She gaped as two painted ladies in large plumed hats flounced toward her. Both had curls past their shoulders, one was blonde and the other cocoa brown, and apple-red lips and cheeks. Their dresses outlandishly pretty, but low cut, exposed cleavage from their full bosoms. One dress was slate blue with white ruffles skirting the bottom, the other a similar design, but pink.

"Hello, missy," the blonde woman spurted. "We need your help with corsets."

Corsets? Hattie had no idea how corsets worked. They sold an assortment in the store and she had viewed the advertisements, but to advise? She followed the women to the underwear section, but stood back.

The blonde woman held a corset against her breast. "Well?" she asked her friend.

"You might earn extra wearing that," the friend said, and turned to Hattie. "What do you think?"

Hattie shook her head, feeling heat rushing to her cheeks. "I-I-I..."

"If these don't work out, can we bring them back?" the blonde asked.

Hattie paused. She didn't know the policy, but they were undergarments. "Only if you d-d-don't wear them."

"Not for long," the blonde chuckled. She winked at Hattie. "I'm kidding. I'd only be trying it on to see how it enhances. Maybe even get a man's point of view."

"Oh," said Hattie, wanting this conversation to end. She had heard of painted ladies, but had never met any. And now to be conversing with some didn't seem real. Her mother always preached the Bible and occasionally remarked that these women were fallen souls. Of course, her mother's second cousin Harold would quietly add: "Wouldn't mind if one of those souls fell on me." And not surprisingly, his comments were only heard by Hattie. She always squirmed and never asked for explanation because she knew he'd provide it.

"I like that frilly one," the brown-haired woman said. "Bet it would pay for itself in one night."

Similar remarks continued while Hattie wrote up their sale. By the time the women left, Hattie's nerves were so frayed, she raced to the front door, bolted it, and beelined back to the counter, slumping down behind it to the floor, breathing slow and deep. After a bit, she heard the front door rattle. Her chest tightened. She grabbed her knees, rocked back and forth, and mouthed,

"G-G-Go away." The door rattled again and she froze, thinking if she didn't move, they'd leave. Suddenly, *ding-a-ling* from the doorbell indicated an opening door and then a man's *hello* and shuffling feet.

Hattie sighed under her breath, gripped the counter, and pulled herself up. "Sorry, I d-d-didn't hear the...door."

"Bolt got stuck," the older man said, "but I jarred it loose. You might have more customers. Saw some ladies heading this way." He grinned and extended his hand. "Name's John Connell."

He had a friendly smile beneath a gray mustache and an easy-going look: beige shirt, dark canvas pants, and suspenders.

"Ivar told me you know about cows."

Hattie furrowed her brow.

"I invented a cow hopple," he said.

"I'm s-s-sorry, this is a high-end...store. They wouldn't carry your product."

"Not asking. The Economy Store will be doing that. I'm looking for cow advice."

"Wh-wh-what?" Before Mr. Connell could explain, Hattie heard the bell and turned to watch four women bustle through the door. She gulped.

"Where are your refined hankies?" a woman asked. "Need them for gift baskets." Hattie pointed to the shelf.

Mr. Connell looked back and forth. He leaned toward Hattie. "Are you alone?"

She nodded nervously.

"Worried about that stammer, aren't you? Did you

bolt that door on purpose?" She gazed down at the counter. He tapped his fingers on the glass forcing her to look at him. "You'll be fine. Follow my lead."

The women hurried over with eight of Hattie's handkerchiefs and plopped them down. "These are the loveliest I've ever seen," a redheaded woman said. "When are you getting more?"

Before Hattie could answer, Mr. Connell interrupted. "Appears she has a bout of laryngitis, but I'm guessing she can answer with a note."

Hattie sheepishly gazed at Mr. Connell, grabbed a tablet, and scribbled out *one dollar.*

"For all eight?"

Mr. Connell interjected again. "Believe she told me twenty cents each. Eight would be a dollar-sixty."

"That sounds fair," the woman said, counting out the money and placing it on the counter. "When's the next order expected?" she asked again.

Hattie gave Mr. Connell a panicked stare.

"Next week?" he asked Hattie.

Hattie paused, remembering that the store reorder was expected to arrive by then. She nodded.

"I'll stop back. Come-on, girls, got a trolley to catch."

"Let me get the door for you," Mr. Connell said. "So what's the big ruckus with all you dressed-up ladies?"

Hattie had been wondering the same thing, but she was too self-conscious to ask.

"We're heading to a catered event in Aberdeen with a fashion show. Over fifty women are expected," the woman said, following her friends out the door.

Hattie grinned at Mr. Connell as he approached. "Wish I'd thought of... laryngitis," she said. "It would've s-s-saved me earlier."

"Did you have a run-in with uppity women?"

"S-s-some," she said, referring to Mrs. Cushman and Mrs. Wiggins. The other women seemed fine, and the painted ladies were nice enough too, but their conversations sent her over the barrel.

"Uppity is not the best of human nature," he said, "but don't let it get you down." He studied Hattie's face. "You look prideful of that sale. What's the story?"

"I made those h-h-handkerchiefs, but they were only shelf fillers...the real ones arrive next w-w-week, never thought anyone w-w-would... buy mine."

"Appears yours are nicer. You should've charged more. How much are you taking for a profit?"

"N-n-nothing. Mine are homemade."

"And the preferred product. Don't ever undersell your worth. Subtract the cost of the material and split the profit between you and the store."

Hattie nodded, but had no intention to follow his advice. "You had a q-q-question about cows?"

He pulled out his drawing. "Can't seem to get the fitting right against the skin. After I told Ivar my dilemma, he immediately thought of you."

Hattie studied the hopple design. "Wh-wh-what material are you using for the straps?"

"Rope."

"Use something softer like p-p-pig or deer skin."

"Great idea. I'll let you know if it works out. If you

make more of those kerchiefs, put me down for some. I have four daughters."

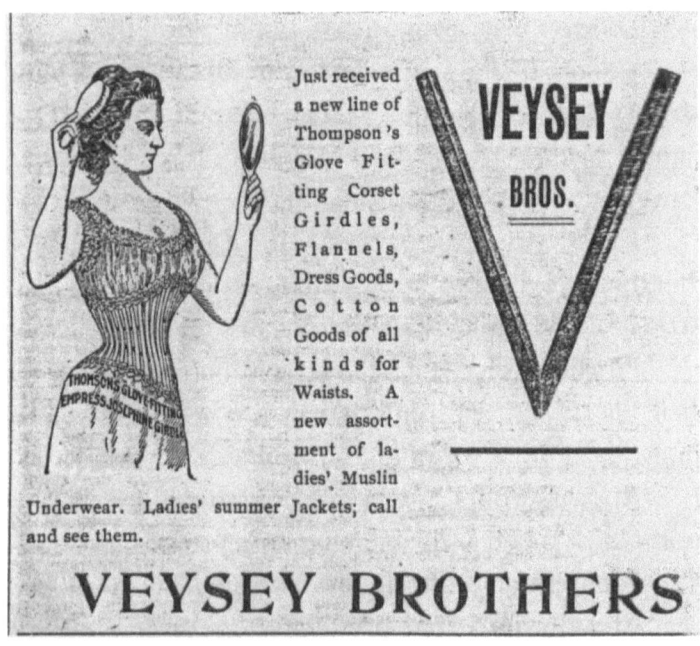

Figure 6
(Courtesy of Veysey Family Collection)

CHAPTER FIVE

OVER THE NEXT three days, the rain hadn't let up and only a handful of customers had come into the store.

"Good morning, Hattie," Mr. Connell said, stomping his feet on the doormat. He shuffled into the store and plopped his cow hopple down on the counter.

"So this is your n-n-new...design," said Hattie.

"Sure is. Wanted you to be the first to see it with pig skin. Works like butter to bread." He surveyed the store. "Awful quiet in here."

"It's been slow. I have something for you." She hurried to the stockroom and returned with four handkerchiefs. "These are a g-g-gift. I insist."

"My daughters will love these, thank you. Nettie and my son-in-law own the Economy Store. I bet they'd sell these for you."

"No. I only make them for f-f-friends."

Just then, Ivar walked through the door and joined them at the front counter. He picked up the cow hopple and examined it. "It turned out nice."

"I used Hattie's suggestion," said Mr. Connell. "Look at these hankies she made for me," showing them to Ivar. "Speaking of hankies, did you finish that red-headed woman's order?"

"Yes, but...I'm p-p-praying that she forgets."

"Why's that?" asked Mr. Connell.

"They weren't m-m-meant to be sold. Besides, Mrs. Bailey's returning tomorrow... and she has a way of c-cconvincing customers to buy…other products. They'll forget about my hankies."

"You better be prepared," he said. "That woman seemed awful headstrong about wanting yours."

Hattie shrugged and hoped that wouldn't be the case. "I'm glad your cow hopple…worked out."

"Me too. Best be on my way and let you young people visit." He turned to Ivar, patted his shoulder, and whispered. "Awful pretty girl, ain't she?"

Ivar responded with an awkward grin, watching as Mr. Connell walked out, and then stepped closer. "What's the story with this headstrong woman?"

"It was an accident," said Hattie, explaining the ordeal of her hankies. "Please don't tell… Josie."

"Why would you think I would? She's not my girlfriend. Oh, she'd like to be and my mother would be so pleased, but Josie's got suitors all over town."

Hattie nodded. She had seen a handful vying for Josie's attention, but none as handsome as Ivar.

"Besides, I prefer this look." He pulled the sleeve of his red-plaid shirt. "If she had her way, I'd be wearing tweed suits every day."

"You look n-n-nice both ways," Hattie said, feeling her cheeks burn. She couldn't imagine him any more handsome than he was now in his flannel shirt, canvas pants, and tousled blond hair.

He smiled and leaned forward on the counter, keeping his blue eyes locked onto hers. "I'd like to get to know you better. What did you do for fun in Wisconsin?"

Hattie's heart raced. She knew he was flirting, and as much as it scared her, it thrilled her too. She took a deep breath and held his gaze. "Social g-g-gatherings. We'd talk and listen to music."

"So, you like music?" Hattie nodded. "Perhaps you'd accompany me to the Opera House?"

Neither had heard the tiny bell announcing an opening door, until Josie blurted, "What's going on?"

Ivar winked at Hattie and spun around. "Hello, Josie."

"Were you waiting for me?" she asked excitedly.

"Nope. Actually, I'm trying to persuade your aunt to go out with me."

A scowl crossed Josie's face as she bore her eyes at Hattie.

Hattie quickly interjected. "No. He's kidding." She was hoping to squelch the wrath she feared would be coming.

Josie feigned a smile. "Ivar, you're such a teaser. Perhaps, I can walk home with you? I have a gift for your mother."

"Give it to me. I'll take it to her."

"No," Josie said. "I'm seeing her tomorrow."

Hattie cleared her throat. "I b-b-better get upstairs and start supper."

Soon as Hattie walked around the counter, Ivar latched onto her arm. "I'll walk you," he said. "You never answered me. Do we have a date?"

Hattie glanced at Josie and saw her eyes harden into an angry glare. Once they got a good distance, she peered over her shoulder and caught Josie's attentive stare again. "What are you doing?" Hattie whispered to Ivar. "You know she's upset."

"Don't care. I've seen the way she treats you. Besides, I figured you needed an escape." He squeezed her arm. "I'll try to stop by tomorrow, so we can finalize our plans."

Hattie nodded, and then she grabbed the banister and raced up the stairs.

JOSIE HAD disappeared before breakfast, and the night before, had eaten supper in her room, stating she had a headache. Hattie concluded that Josie was still stewing over Ivar's earlier behavior, but Josie skipping family meals wasn't unusual either. Several mornings, she had met friends before school, and three to four times during the past two weeks, had dined with different families.

Much as Hattie didn't want to admit it, she welcomed Josie's absence from the table. Today, with Mrs. Bailey returning to work, Hattie was on edge and quite relieved when Mabs announced that Josie had already left. After Hattie got the girls off to school, she stood at the full-length oval mirror, neatly pinned back her dark-brown curls to cascade down her back, and turned side to side checking her outline in her new rose-colored dress. Modest as she was, Hattie was pleased with her new appearance. Thoughts of Ivar liking it too raced through her head and she was excited to see him.

Descending the stairs to the store, Hattie caught Josie and Mrs. Bailey huddled at the counter in a private chatter and paused on a step, contemplating turning around until she saw Josie glance up at her. Josie cupped her hand around her mouth and whispered to Mrs. Bailey. When Mrs. Bailey looked over her shoulder, Hattie knew that she had been their morning topic. Her chest tightened as she slowly walked down the stairs.

Josie picked up her books. "See you this afternoon," she told Mrs. Bailey and hurried toward the door. Mrs. Bailey strode toward Hattie.

Hattie had practiced all morning without a stutter, but now she feared what would spurt out. She paused. "G-g-good..."

Mrs. Bailey held up her hand. "Don't strain your words. You'll work in the stockroom today." Just as she started to instruct, the front door opened, striking the bell *ding-a-ling*, which sent Mrs. Bailey clip-clopping away.

Startled by Mrs. Bailey's shrill voice instead of her usual cheerful customer tone, Hattie turned around and watched Mrs. Bailey chastising a sandy-haired boy. Her voice carried like a megaphone.

"Don't you have any common sense?" Mrs. Bailey snapped.

The young man piped back. "I told you, it won't fit through the back door."

Mrs. Bailey threw her hands into the air. "Wait here," she said. She spun around, caught Hattie's gaze, and thumbed at the young man. "Take care of that," she told Hattie, and then she strutted to the front counter.

"Hello," said Hattie, approaching the boy. "San Fran...cisco," reading the stamped name on the crate.

"Yep," he said. "It came in on a clipper ship."

She led him to the back through the long velvet curtain dividing the sales floor from the stockroom.

Whenever Hattie had downtime, she'd knit until Mrs. Bailey requested her help. When the young man removed the crate from his handcart and pushed it against the wall, its edge caught Hattie's knitting basket and knocked it to the floor.

The boy stooped over. "What nice socks," he said, examining them closer as he shoveled the loose items back into the basket. "Perfect thickness."

"For my brother in W-W-Wisconsin," said Hattie.

"What I wouldn't give to have some like these. One thing about workin' on the docks, freezin' feet."

"If you open the crate... f-f-for me, I'll give you a pair."

His lopsided smile widened, baring slightly crisscrossed front teeth, which Hattie determined complemented his boyish looks.

"Gray or bl-bl-black?"

"It'd be awful nice to have both. I'd pay extra for them. Good socks are hard to find."

She handed him both pair. "Keep your money."

"Really?" he said, stuffing the socks into his deep pocket. "You sure are nicer than that old shrew."

Hattie flattened her lips, quelling a chuckle.

"Best get movin'," he said. "Thanks again. If you ever need a favor, give a holler. I'm Olli."

Hattie smiled and nodded.

BY EARLY AFTERNOON, Hattie had emptied the crate and organized and inventoried all of the new items. Time to head upstairs, she decided. On her way to the staircase, which led to the upstairs apartment, she spotted Josie talking to a customer. She didn't think anything about it until she heard their raised voices.

"No," the woman said, "the ones with the fancy embroidering."

Hattie gasped when she saw red hair sticking out from under the customer's hat. Her stomach wrenched. *Oh, no. Is that about my hankies?*

"We don't carry that style," Josie blurted.

"Yes, you do," the woman insisted.

Hattie knew if she started up the stairs, she'd be seen. The same was true if she tried to make it back to the stockroom, so she darted to the nearest clothing rack, crouched down behind it, and watched.

Josie waved Mrs. Bailey over.

"Yes?" said Mrs. Bailey, coming toward them.

"I ordered more of these hankies," the woman said, showing the hankie to Mrs. Bailey.

"Not here, you didn't," Josie interjected with a snotty tone.

The woman let out an exasperated sigh. "I'm not daft. Where's the other young lady who works here?"

Josie looked at Mrs. Bailey, then both aimed their eyes toward the stockroom. Hattie could see that they were debating whether to summon her. She gathered her courage, stepped from behind the clothing rack, and walked toward them.

When the customer saw Hattie, she stomped over to her, waving the hankie in her hand. "You remember me, don't you, miss?" the woman asked. "And these handkerchiefs?"

Hattie sheepishly nodded.

Mrs. Bailey reprimanded Hattie with a stern stare. "You do?"

"Yes," said Hattie, "but..."

"Do you have more of these handkerchiefs in the stockroom?" Mrs. Bailey asked.

Hattie nodded again.

"Get them, please," said Mrs. Bailey in a firm tone.

Hattie returned with the ten handkerchiefs she had made for this customer.

After Mrs. Bailey scrutinized Hattie's work, she handed the hankies to the woman. "Please accept my apology. I didn't realize a different line had arrived. We'll give you a *free* hankie for all of the confusion."

"That's the least you can do," the redhead huffed. "I'd like ten more. How soon can I get them?"

All eyes turned to Hattie again. "Uh, uh."

"Do you have more in stock?" Mrs. Bailey asked.

"No," answered Hattie.

Mrs. Bailey turned to the customer again. "We're not getting more, but you can have all ten of these at no cost."

"Really?" the woman said.

"Yes," said Mrs. Bailey. She cupped the customer's elbow and escorted her to the door, reiterating apologies all the way.

When the women got out of earshot, Josie narrowed her eyes. "You made those, didn't you?"

Hattie took a deep breath "Y-y-yes, but..."

"How dare you," Josie yelped.

Soon as the door closed, Mrs. Bailey rushed over. "Hush," she told Josie. "Your voice carries."

"Her handkerchiefs are homemade," said Josie. "She had no right to sell them in our store."

Hattie spoke up. "Th-th-they were...shelf fillers until the r-r-real order arrived."

"Th-th-th," Josie repeated. "You can't even talk right. You're such an embarrassment, and the way you've thrown yourself at Ivar, what a farce. He's only mocking you, probably has a bet going with friends on how fast he can snag the stuttering girl. I assure you that he won't be seen in public with you. His mother will make certain of that."

"Enough," Mrs. Bailey demanded.

Josie stared at Mrs. Bailey. "You can't imagine what it's like being related to her. Think I want people knowing that she's my aunt? She's a joke all over town." Josie stepped toward Hattie, fire in her voice. "I can't wait until you leave."

Struggling back tears, Hattie quickened her steps toward the door. With Josie's hateful words echoing in her head, she wondered if Josie might be right about Ivar. He seemed nice, but she really didn't know him. She did know that young men could be cruel, recalling James from the neighboring town at a local dance. She had danced with him most of the night. When she returned from freshening up, she had heard him mimicking her stuttering with his friends. Hattie shook off the memory and hastened her steps.

With her mind wandering in all directions and wetness blurring her vision, Hattie didn't notice the dark-haired woman bent over fiddling with her boot, until she collided into her. "I'm sooo s-s-sorry," Hattie said, grabbing the woman's arm. "Are you...all right?"

The plump woman caught her balance and laughed. "It serves me right for blocking the walkway," she said, straightening up and looking at Hattie square on. "Are those tears I see?" Hattie shook her head. "Something's got you in a pother. Maybe I can help?"

"I'm fine," said Hattie, trying not to gawk at the colorful woman wearing a fuzzy blue boa, bright shamrock-green coat, and a blue and green ostrich-feathered hat. Her face wasn't painted like the painted ladies, nor did she flounce when she walked, Hattie later learned, but she sure was flamboyant.

"Did a man cause those tears?" the woman continued, sliding her round glasses back up on her nose.

"N-n-no," said Hattie.

"My house is on the next street. You can gather your wits with a cup of tea." Before Hattie could respond, the woman looped her arm through Hattie's and pulled her along.

"B-b-but," Hattie tried to say.

The woman ignored her and talked about her day as she quick-stepped Hattie for three more blocks before stopping in front of a yellow Victorian house.

"Here we are," she said.

The house was as vibrant as the woman was with its lavender-lace curtains hanging in the dormer windows and purple, blue, and green pillows, all shapes and sizes, nicely placed in chairs scattered across the wrap-around porch. A large black sign with yellow lettering hung from the porch beam:

DAPHANIE'S BOARDING HOUSE

"I d-d-don't recognize this p-p-part of town."

"Finn Town," the woman answered.

Hattie's mouth popped open, remembering Ivar's warning about Finn Town the day she had arrived—to stay clear of it, especially at night.

"F-F-Finn Town?" repeated Hattie.

"So, you've heard the rumors? It's all true, but no worries. Finn Town doesn't turn raucous until the mill workers get off work. We've got hours before that. My name's Daphanie, and who might you be?"

"H-H-Hattie."

CHAPTER SIX

WHILE HATTIE SIPPED her tea, Daphanie spilled her story. She was born in Minnesota, an only child, and lost her mother when she was twelve. After her mother died, she and her father headed west.

"My father treated me like a princess," she said with a twinge of sadness in her voice. "Truthfully, he feared I'd never snag a man. Before he died, he bought this boarding house and put it in my name. Now I'm a thirty-year-old mongoose who only answers to herself. And I like it that way."

Her apple-shaped cheeks and wide grin showed such friendliness that Hattie couldn't help but smile.

"I'm guessing your stuttering is the cause of your upset? At least, part of it?"

Hattie froze, wishing Daphanie hadn't brought it up.

"No need to tell me." Lifting her skirt, she showed a deformed leg. "Happened right after we moved here, chopping wood. Doctor Stevens said I was lucky. Still functions, it's just wobbly going up and down the stairs."

"I'm s-s-sorry."

"Not looking for sympathy. Point I'm trying to make is we all have vexations, of some sort."

As they talked, Hattie realized they had a lot in common: both Midwest girls brought up on a farm by Bible-teaching mothers and a love of music. Hattie had mastered the piano by age eight. Daphanie learned early too. They determined it a good skill to have, especially during cold winters.

"Come by any time," said Daphanie. "Maybe we can play a duet."

"I'd like that," Hattie said, standing and setting her cup on the tray. "You're so k-k-kind."

"Kindness doesn't cost a penny. Too bad others don't use it more often."

THE NEXT AFTERNOON, Hattie avoided Josie. Josie stayed her distance, too. When Mabs cornered Josie in the store, neither girl was aware that Hattie was in the back stocking shelves.

"What'd you do to Aunt Hattie?" Mabs said. "I can tell by the way you're both acting that something's wrong. I'm guessing it came from you. You better spill it or else."

Josie huffed. "Did you know she's been selling her own handkerchiefs in the store, using our supplies, and keeping all the profits?"

How dare she, I'm not a thief! Hattie stomped toward her nieces. "I did no s-s-such thing," she said, trying to censor her anger. "Those h-h-handkerchiefs were shelf warmers. I had no idea the women would buy them, let alone order m-m-more."

Josie sneered. "And where did you get your supplies?"

"I brought the h-h-handkerchiefs with me from Wisconsin. I gave all the profits...to the s-s-store."

"You should have split the profits," said Mabs. "I bet Father would agree."

Josie glared at her sister. "Keep Father out of this. Her homemade hankies are not reputable." She turned to Hattie. "You better not try anything like that again." She raised her chin in the air and strutted toward the front counter.

Mabs sighed. "She can be such a snit and never admits when she's wrong. Mother and Father would be furious at how she's acting toward you."

"I know," said Hattie, "but we'll k-k-keep this to ourselves. There's no r-r-reason to upset your parents. Besides, I'm not making...the hankies anymore."

"Tomorrow is Saturday and Mrs. Bailey and Josie will be handling the store," said Mabs. "Why don't you come with me on deliveries?"

Hattie paused. "I'd like that. Let's bring Tillie and Eva along. I'll pack a lunch."

ON DELIVERY DAY, Hattie sat next to Mabs on the bench seat and Eva and Tillie rode in the covered bed with the supplies. Whenever Josie and her words crept into Hattie's head, she shooed them away.

The wooded countryside on the rutted roads reminded Hattie of Wisconsin, and for a moment made her homesick. Every delivery they made was so grateful to see them that it reaffirmed her faith in kindness and mended her heart a bit too. One family even gave them a cherry pie. "This is our last stop," Mabs announced, heading the wagon into a rundown farm. Two young girls and four boys circled their wagon. Eva and Tillie looked out from the back and waved to the children.

"Whoa," said Mabs, yanking on Teaspoon's reins. A slender woman walked out of the house and up to their wagon.

"Hi, Mrs. Matthews," said Mabs. "This is my aunt, Hattie."

The woman nodded to Hattie, then she whispered to Mabs, but loud enough for Hattie to hear. "I only have ten dollars. Could some of this go on account? If not, I'll sort through it."

Mabs looked at Hattie and frowned.

Hattie cleared her throat. "D-d-do you know when you might be able to pay?"

"Hopefully next week if my husband sells more beaver hides. He's in Aberdeen now bartering a deal."

Hattie knew from Mrs. Bailey that credit was rarely offered, but she also knew every rule had exceptions. She glanced at the raggedy children again, then back to their mother. "That sounds f-f-fine. So, you'll owe six dollars on account," Hattie told Mrs. Matthews and adjusted the receipt.

Mabs interjected. "I'll stop by next week to collect." Mabs turned to Hattie and whispered. "Bet their family would enjoy that cherry pie."

"I think so...too."

The woman's smile widened as Mabs handed her the pie. She glanced at Hattie with tears now pooling in her eyes. "Thank you both."

After they pulled onto the road again, Mabs turned to Hattie. "Good thing you were here to make that decision. On my last delivery, I extended them credit.

Josie had a fit, telling me that I'd better never allow it again."

"Did they pay?"

"Yes, but a week late."

"S-s-seemed the right thing...to do," said Hattie. "I'll advance the six dollars now." She reached into her pocket and handed Mabs the money.

"Thank you, Aunt Hattie. I wasn't looking forward to hearing another lecture from Josie."

Instead of responding, Hattie lifted her eyes toward the sky. "Looks like rain, smells like it too."

"We'll take the short-cut home," said Mabs, pulling off onto a dirt road.

As the wagon's springboard creaked along the uneven path, Hattie looked up at the threatening sky. Suddenly, as if the clouds had split open, they heaved into a downpour, drenching Hattie and Mabs' hair and clothes.

Eva and Tillie poked their heads out the front opening. "Back inside," Mabs told them.

"Yes," Hattie affirmed as sideways rain doused them more.

Hattie cinched her coat collar tighter and shivered from the wetness soaking through to her dress. Even poor Teaspoon looked a fright—the horse's bushy mane was matted and her fluffy tail a stringy mess. She glanced at Mabs. "Should we s-s-stop and w-w-wait out the storm?"

"No place to pull off," Mabs said, keeping the reins tight and forcing Teaspoon to trot through mud puddles now splashing onto the horse's long legs and up to Hattie's boots and coat.

The road had turned into a muddy slush. Teaspoon whinnied, trying to pull her legs up as quicksand-like mud sucked the wagon down.

Hattie looked at Mabs. "We're st-st-stuck. Hand me the reins."

"You don't know horses," Mabs said.

"But...I do," said Hattie. "I was raised on a farm."

Mabs shook her head. "No, I'll get us out of this." She slapped the reins up and down.

The horse tried lifting one leg at a time, but it appeared useless with such a heavy load. "Come on, Teaspoon," Mabs cried out, gently slapping the reins again. The horse slugged forward, but only an inch or so before the back wheel snapped in two.

The wagon plummeted to its side.

The younger girls let out blood-curdling screams.

"Watch out," Hattie shrieked, sliding sideways off the seat. She grabbed hold of the sideboard, which kept her upright, landing her feet first in the mud, but it splashed up to her face and onto the front of her coat.

Mabs released her hold on Teaspoon's reins as she slid off the wagon. Hattie tried to catch her, but she was coming too fast. She plunged into the muck.

Hattie reached down and pulled Mabs up. "Are you all right?"

"Yes," she said, wiping mud from her face with her hand, "but the wheel's broken."

"I see," said Hattie.

Mabs slogged toward Teaspoon. Hattie headed to the back of the wagon, tugged the curtain open, and found Eva and Tillie huddled together. "Hope you're both okay." They nodded in unison. Eva crawled out first. Once Hattie got her off the wagon and into the mud, she turned to Tillie, who immediately climbed into Hattie's arms.

As Hattie carried her niece, Eva grasped onto to Hattie's skirt and the two of them footslogged toward the drier ground where Mabs was now standing with the horse, untangling its twisted reins.

Mabs glanced at Hattie and shamefully looked away. "I'm sorry. Sometimes I can be so stubborn. Mother scolds me about it all the time."

"It's all...right. The wagon can be f-f-fixed and no one's hurt, n-n-not even Teaspoon."

Mabs' lip quivered as she nodded.

"You must be freezing," said Hattie. "Let's find a dry place...and get out of these wet clothes."

After retrieving the picnic basket and supplies out of the wagon, they attached what they could to Teaspoon's saddle and covered it with a canvas tarp.

"How far back to the Matthews' farm?" Hattie asked.

"Too far," said Mabs, "and it's too muddy to walk."

"Any other ideas?"

Mabs sighed. "There's an old graveyard with a burial vault up the road."

Hattie gulped. "Gr-gr-graveyard?" Hattie hated stark darkness, and as a child had nightmares, which she never fully outgrew.

Tillie piped up, "Oh, no, that's where ghosts live."

"I don't want to go there, either," Eva said, speaking louder than Hattie had ever heard her talk.

"Mabs, there must be somewhere else," said Hattie.

"None that I know of out here," Mabs answered. "It's either that or the woods."

Hattie thought and seriously considered the woods, but it had its demons too, wolves and cougars to name a couple. "Girls," she said, "Th-th-there's nothing to fear. Come along."

CHAPTER SEVEN

HEADSTONES BLOTTED the landscape like gapped teeth. Some were heart-shaped, others towering monument types or wooden crosses, and even more unusual shapes. Hattie held her younger nieces' hands and followed Mabs to the moss-covered tomb. It reminded Hattie of an old gothic church.

"Are there dead people in there?" Tillie asked.

Not wanting to scare her young nieces more, Hattie spoke in a confident tone. "It's safe," she said.

Mabs and Hattie pushed on the heavy door. The rusty hinges creaked as it partially opened. Hattie stepped into the murky room, shivered from the icy coldness, and gagged from the foul odor. Covering her mouth with her hand, she turned to Mabs. "We'll camp outside."

Standing on the tomb's steps, Hattie scanned the cemetery. The rain had let up. She pointed to an old-growth cedar with two grave markers underneath. "Over there." She grabbed Tillie's hand, carried the picnic basket in her other, and stomped toward the giant tree. Mabs and Eva followed with Teaspoon and tethered her to a branch.

"This t-t-tree must be over...two-hundred-years old," Hattie remarked, looking up and up, "and at least thirty feet of bare trunk. See how the tall branches shield l-l-like an umbrella, keeping the ground...dry underneath. And there's p-p-plenty of room to build a small fire."

"But there are graves here," Eva squeaked.

Hattie nodded and placed the picnic basket to the ground. "Yes, and I'm g-g-guessing they were nice people like us and won't mind sharing." Hattie didn't like sitting there either, but it was far better than the dark tomb. "Uncle Wallace and I got c-c-caught once in a storm and camped under...a tree. Wallace taught me what...to do." She didn't admit that her older brother had done most of the work, but nonetheless, she watched as he instructed.

Releasing Tillie's hand, Hattie knelt down to the picnic basket and pulled out matches. Uneaten sandwiches and apples were in the basket too. "We need dry k-k-kindling. Anything th-th-that will burn—twigs, branches, pinecones."

Eva and Tillie scoured the woods with Hattie. Cradling pinecones in their lifted-up skirts, they waddled back to the campsite and dumped their findings onto the sheltered ground. Hattie pulled dry blankets off Teaspoon's back, spread one out on the ground, and handed the other two to the children.

Hattie spotted Mabs coming out of the brush with twigs and bark stuffed into her wet overall pockets and branches in her arms. Mabs raced to the campsite, dropping the branches at Hattie's feet. "Hope these are still dry too," she said, pulling out the kindling she had tucked into her pockets.

Scraping the pine needles off to one side, Hattie tossed away the wet pieces and picked up the dry ones. Placing the twigs upright, she formed a tiny stick-figure teepee-like tent. Good as Wallace's, she determined as she sprinkled dry tinder inside and lit the fire. "Smell the evergreen," she told the children. "It's the p-p-pinecones that give off the scent." After the fire glowed, Hattie peeled off her wet dress, boots, and socks, and snuggled close to Tillie under her blanket. Wetness hadn't saturated through to Hattie's petticoat and she was grateful for that. She was also thankful that the younger girls' dresses had stayed dry, but Mabs was soaked and refused to strip. "Toss those w-w-wet clothes toward the fire," Hattie insisted.

Mabs reluctantly obeyed, then slid under Eva's blanket. Eva puckered her lips. "Your feet are cold," she said. Hattie chuckled in silence. It was the first time that even-tempered Eva had ever showed annoyance.

As the sky darkened from the storm, the children huddled next to Hattie. She tried to stay calm, but her imagination played tricks. The tree branches shadowing over headstones reminded her of ghoulish arms. Her gaze traveled to the burial tomb, so cold and stark, and the eeriness of knowing bodies were buried inside chewed at her gut. What a terrible place to be stranded, she thought as she looked at the children, seeing fear in their eyes that she hoped they weren't seeing in hers. She knew dusk would approach in a few hours, then pitch-blackness.

Tillie bit her lip. "Aunt Hattie, I'm scared."

Hattie pulled her close. "You're safe."

"Nice people are buried here," Eva added. "Aunt Hattie said so," and then she recited a senseless verse: *Betty Beedee bit a bite of bitter butter bread.*

"What's that?" Hattie asked her.

"She makes up tongue twisters," Mabs said, "but never figured she'd use a tombstone to conjure up one."

Hattie turned around and read the marker:

Beatrice Beedee—March 5, 1885
Loving Wife of Arnold
Mother of Theo and Jane

Hattie winked at Eva. "So, she ate bitter butter bread?" said Hattie. For unknown reasons, tongue twisters always rolled off Hattie's tongue without a stutter.

The children snickered.

"What did you do in Wisconsin?" asked Eva.

"I was a d-d-dairymaid," Hattie said. "I milked cows, skimmed c-c-cream, filled f-f-food troughs and cleaned."

"Cows?" said Tillie. "How many?"

"Forty. Holsteins, Guernseys, and Jerseys. After my b-b-brothers moved west, Mother hired full-time farmhands, but I still tended to Bessie."

Hattie explained that Bessie, a brown and white Jersey, had been under her care since a calf. Her stories lifted their moods until a piercing howl ricocheted through the trees.

"What was that?" said Tillie, grabbing Hattie.

When another high-pitched "*Y...o...w...l...*," echoed, Hattie stiffened and the hair on the back of her neck prickled. The children stared wide-eyed at their aunt.

"I d-d-don't know," Hattie stammered, her heart thumping so hard she was sure she might faint. "Maybe c-c-coyotes." *Coyotes usually don't come out until night and they don't like fire, unless they're hungry.* "Cover your h-h-heads with the blankets and keep low."

After another howl, she determined it had to be pranksters or something else, but with a darkening sky, she feared the fire could be a beacon, leading who or whatever straight to them.

"Put out the f-f-fire," she said, feeling uneasy as she threw on wet pine needles, smothering the flame.

"Could they be ghosts?" Tillie asked, trembling.

"No," Hattie reassured. "All the n-n-nice people buried here are in H-H-Heaven."

"All of them?" Tillie said. "Are you sure?"

"It'll be fine. N-n-no more questions." Truth was Hattie had run out of answers and was as scared as the girls were, but didn't want to show it. She pulled her wet socks and boots on, draped her soiled dress over her arm, and leaped to her feet. "Come on. Get behind the t-t-tree."

Mabs grabbed her boots and overalls.

"What about werewolves?" Eva said. Her voice quivered as she peeked around the tree. "I see three silhouettes and they have beards like wolves."

"Hush, Eva," said Hattie. "That's just f-f-folklore."

"Hattie," Mabs whispered, her voice now shaking. "I brought Father's rifle from the wagon. It's tied to Teaspoon. Do you know how to shoot?"

Hattie gulped. She'd shot a rifle plenty, but her targets were tin cans and stumps, not unknowns who howled. Peeking from behind the tree again, they saw three figures nearing the vault. In their shadows, axes and picks hung over their shoulders. "*Y...o...w...l,*" cried out again, then a man's commanding voice, "Enough. Don't need you wakin' the spooks."

The girls watched the men push the heavy door and then prop it open. With kerosene light pouring out, the tomb looked like an evil jack-o-lantern—orange inside and emitting sinister light through the broken windows, like devilish eyes. Hattie bit her lip and shuddered.

Moments later...*pound...pound...pound...*

Suddenly, branches cracked from the forest behind them. They spun around and crowded closer together.

"What's that noise?" Eva asked, grasping onto Hattie's leg.

"Shhh...," Hattie whispered, quivering as she listened. She grabbed the rifle and pointed it at the dark figure coming toward them.

A man called out. "Mabs...Mabs...are you out here?"

Mabs' mouth dropped open. "It's Ivar."

Still shaking, Hattie lowered the gun and watched him come closer.

"Out on a cold rainy day, on this road without a man?" Ivar said, "Whose hair-brained idea was that?"

Hattie slowly stepped forward. "I take f-f-full responsibility. Mabs would have been h-h-home hours ago if we hadn't slowed her down...for a picnic."

He paused, appearing embarrassed by his remark. "Our logging camp is several miles up the road," he said. "If we leave right now, we can reach it before total darkness."

Eva piped up. "What about the grave robbers? Do we have to pass them? They're in the vault. They look like werewolves."

"Is that right?" he said, gazing in the direction of the robbers. "Not the first time, but I'll put the scare in them to make it their last."

"Now?" said Hattie.

"No. I'll get you to my wagon first," he said. "But the only way to get the horse out of here is to pass the crypt. Best we stay together."

Hattie grabbed Eva's hand and reached for Tillie's, but Tillie already had her fingers clenched onto Hattie's petticoat. "Ivar will p-p-protect us," Hattie whispered, "but we have to be quiet...as field mice."

The girls followed Ivar along the edge of the woods, tiptoeing around graves. Mabs behind them lead the horse. Hattie's heart thumped clear up to her throat.

Teaspoon sputtered.

"Shhh...," Mabs said, petting the horse's nose.

"Hear that?" a robber said, coming to the doorway.

"Get down," Ivar whispered, motioning with his hand. Luckily, branches shielded them from the man's view. Even Teaspoon was blocked behind a bush. It seemed forever before the robber stepped back into the vault.

Once they got to a clearing, they bolted toward the road. Mabs guided Teaspoon by her bridle as Ivar trailed behind, walking backwards with his gun. When they reached his wagon, he held up his lantern and lifted out a small package wrapped in a burlap sack.

"Stand back and hold the horses," he said.

"What are you doing?" Mabs asked.

"Firecrackers from last year's Fourth of July. Good that I saved a few. Cover your ears."

Lighting the fuse, he lobbed the red cylinder high into the air toward the graveyard.

K...a...b...o...o...m..., loud as thunder.

Voices yelled in the distance. "What was that?"

A moment later...*B.a.n.g.*..., shot from Ivar's rifle, then another...*B.a.n.g.*.... Ivar called out. "Posse's on the way."

"Hand me your r-r-rifle," Hattie told Mabs. And without hesitation, she cocked the hammer, pointed the rifle into the air, and fired. Ivar fired again, then Hattie. Three more sequences of Ivar then Hattie, until Ivar's firing stopped. When they heard his footsteps, Hattie held the rifle, just in case, but pointed it to the ground.

"Good backup, Mabs," Ivar said. "They're running like scared rabbits."

"Wasn't me," said Mabs. "It was Aunt Hattie."

CHAPTER EIGHT

OIL LAMPS lit up the shantytown logging camp like a makeshift carnival. The girls followed Ivar into the largest structure. The sign above the door read *Mess Hall*. Inside were tall beamed ceilings and two long wooden tables, stretching twenty feet or so, with benches on each side.

"Wait here. I'll get Bert," said Ivar, hurrying through another doorway that read *Cookhouse* above it. Hoots and whistles echoed from the corner of what appeared to be a Saturday night poker game.

A bony man with bulldog jowls and grayish-thin hair stood at the doorway, wiping his hands on his long white apron. "What's all the hoopla?" he barked. He looked at Hattie and shook his head. "You're the cause."

Hattie's eyes widened. "I-I-I didn't do..."

"It ain't what you did, it's what you are. And a pretty one to boot." He turned to the men. "Plug your mouth-holes." He motioned to the girls. "Come along."

Hattie clutched Eva and Tillie's hands and stepped close behind Mabs as redness crawled up her neck.

"Ivar went to see his pa," the man said. "He told me to get you fed. I'm Bert, the cook." He pointed to tin bowls sitting on a long table heaped with boiled eggs, bread, beans, sliced beef, and blueberries. "Dig in."

"Thanks," said Mabs. "We are starved."

"Take off your coats," he added, "and let 'em hang. It's toasty in here, should dry quick."

Tillie piped up. "But Aunt Hattie's only wearing her petticoat under her coat."

Hattie gasped and turned away from Bert. *Why did she have to reveal that? Thank goodness Ivar wasn't here.*

Mabs interjected. "Her dress is drying on our horse."

"Makes sense," said Bert.

Hattie sighed. "Girls, pl-pl-please."

Bert cleared his throat, "Well...miss, if you need a frock, I should be able to scare one up by mornin'."

Hattie sheepishly nodded as heat rushed to her cheeks. "Th-th-thank you."

While she ate, Hattie scanned the cookhouse. It had three massive wood-burning stoves, washtub-sized pots, pans, and bowls, dangling from beams or stacked here and there, and barrel after barrel of potatoes, grains, and other provisions along the walls.

Bert walked over to their table. "Ivar said your wagon broke a wheel."

"Y-y-yes," Hattie said, swallowing down food.

"Got a flunky shack for you to drop your heads for the night," he said. "Much cleaner than the bunkhouses. Only wish I had flunkies to put in 'em."

"Flunkies?" asked Mabs.

"Helpers for the meals, and they stoke the stoves and clean up around the camp too. Two quit last week. Bein' short-handed has takin' its toll."

"Maybe we can...help you," said Hattie.

"If you were stayin' longer, I'd take you up on that, but not worth the trainin'. Hurry and eat up. The gut hammer rings early." Bert walked back to the stove.

"What's a gut hammer?" Tillie asked.

"It's a triangle b-b-bell," said Hattie. "We used one on the f-f-farm for wake-up calls. They're awful...noisy."

IVAR SAT at his father's desk and calculated estimates for each cut tree based on length and girth. His father walked in and plunked down into a chair.

Ivar was a younger version of his dad—same muscular build, blond and blue-eyed, except Ivar was taller.

"Saw the Veysey girls in the mess hall," Mr. Ekola remarked. "Who's the young miss with them?"

"Hattie," said Ivar. "Mr. Veysey's sister. She helped scare off the robbers at the graveyard."

His father raised an eyebrow. "How'd she do that?"

"Rifle shots, timed after mine. Quite impressive."

"Hmm," his father said, holding back a grin. "Is that all that caught your eye?"

"Not sure what you mean?"

His father chuckled. "Dressing plain doesn't conceal a pretty girl."

Ivar gave his father an awkward grin. "I've noticed."

"Is she being added to your mother's list?"

Ivar rolled his eyes.

"Your mother's already grooming several young ladies for you. Believe Miss Josie is at the top."

"I know and she's pushing me toward law school."

"Last I heard," his father said, "your mother sees you as a lawyer, then mayor, and eventually a congressman."

"I'd rather work with you at the camp."

"And I'd love to have you, son." He paused. "But after Karl's accident, it doesn't seem wise."

Karl, Ivar's older brother, worked at the camp. Two years ago, he was crushed by a falling tree.

Ivar solemnly nodded. "I'm not a daredevil like Karl was. I want to learn engineering to make the equipment better. I could help with management too."

"Maybe once you finish college, but right now your mother has control. As it is, every time you visit here, I get an earful. I doubt if Henrik will ever get within twenty miles of this place." Henrik was Ivar's seventeen-year-old brother.

BERT LED the girls to the flunky shack and bid them goodnight. He had promised clean and that it was: stark-white paneled walls, a rod for hanging clothes, and two thin bunk beds, each with a wool blanket and duck-feathered pillow atop a straw-filled mattress. Eva and Mabs slept in the top bunks. Hattie and Tillie were on the bottom.

Awakened by the clanging gut hammer, Hattie slowly sat up, stretched, and lit the lantern, but kept it low. She looked at her nieces. All were fast asleep. She slipped her soiled dress over her head, secured her hair into a tight bun, and tiptoed over to Mabs.

Mabs opened her eyes to Hattie's gentle shaking. She propped upright on her elbows. "What's wrong?"

"Nothing," said Hattie. "Wanted you to know that I'm going to the c-c-cookhouse. When the girls wake up, b-b-bring them over."

"Okay," Mabs said, plopping back onto the pillow.

Once inside the cookhouse, Hattie stomped her muddy boots on a mat, removed her coat, and then reached for an apron and hair net hanging on a nearby hook. Bert gave her a puzzled look as she tied the apron string behind her back.

"Wh-Wh-What can I do?" she asked.

He scratched his chin. "The donkey punchers are eatin' now," he said, explaining that the donkey punchers had to get the boilers fired up before the cutting crew arrived. "The main rush hits in an hour. Fry up as many spuds as you can."

Hattie peeled and sliced more potatoes, speared the cooked bacon onto a large platter, and then scraped her potatoes and onions into the hot bacon grease. With two hands, she lifted another cast iron skillet off a rack, set it atop the stove, and tossed in more bacon.

Bert walked over and forked out a potato wedge. "Nice touch cookin' these in bacon grease," he said, chewing. "You're quick too. Ever done this before?"

"On our d-d-dairy farm. We have forty cows. It's a lot of work getting the milk to the c-c-creamery. We had to f-f-feed the farmhands first."

"Did you ever milk a cow?"

"Yes, tw-tw-twice a day." She didn't add that before each milking she had to get the cow relaxed, feed it grain, test its teats and check its udder, then spend forty-five minutes or so on a stool, milking. That's if the cow wasn't jumpy and kicked over the can of milk. The stalls had to be cleaned throughout the day too.

He stood beside her, picked up a knife, and started peeling more potatoes. "I was raised on a farm too," he said. "Thumbs up or thumbs down?"

"Up," she said, referring to the grip on the cow's teats.

"Hand milkin' is hard. I recall burnin' forearms."

"Yes," said Hattie.

As Hattie got older, her mother worried about Hattie getting muscular arms from milking the cows, so she transferred Hattie's duties to the cookhouse and to tending to only one cow, Bessie.

Bert pointed to two teenage boys, "Bill and Tom O'Leary, my cookhouse flunkies."

Both boys, thin as string beans, had freckles and curly reddish-brown hair. Hattie guessed them to be no older than fourteen and fifteen.

"Start fillin' the platters," Bert said, scooping his cooked potatoes onto one. Soon as Hattie filled hers, Tom put it in the warming oven and placed an empty one for her to refill.

"Hattie?" Ivar said, walking toward her.

She glanced up, and without missing a stroke, flipped potatoes and onions onto another platter.

"Leave her be," Bert said. "She's got a rhythm goin'."

Ivar stepped back. "Sorry." He headed back to the cookhouse table where his father was sitting, but kept his eyes glued on Hattie.

"And she can cook too," his father said, grinning as he watched his son watching Hattie.

Bert set a plate in front of Mr. Ekola. "Take a taste."

Sampling Hattie's cooking, Mr. Ekola nodded approvingly. Hattie sighed with relief. Ivar had told her that he'd seen men walk off the job, all because of the cook. Bert was considered one of the best.

"Good as yours, Bert," Mr. Ekola remarked. "Watch out, you might get replaced."

"Baaa," he snorted. "Ain't got that kinda luck." He pulled out his pocket watch. "Five-fifteen, time to alert the crew." He stepped outside, and a moment later, deafening gongs of the iron gut-hammer ricocheted throughout the camp. Shortly after, the men single-filed into the mess hall.

Bill and Tom rushed out to the mess hall with coffee pots, raced back into the cookhouse to grab two more, and out again, pouring fast as they could. When they carried out mountain-high platters of eggs, bacon, and potatoes, Bert followed with a pot of beans. Hattie balanced a tray of flapjacks piled so high that she feared it might topple before she got it placed. Within minutes, the room silenced to only forks clanking on the plates and "pass-the-grub" for seconds and thirds. Hattie had never witnessed such a spectacle. Bert touched her shoulder and motioned her back into the cookhouse.

"S-s-surprised it's so quiet in there," she said, referring to the mess hall.

"Eatin' is a serious business. No time for chatter."

Hattie spotted her nieces sitting at the table with Ivar and his father. She hesitated.

"Get goin' before it's gobbled up," Bert said.

Ivar stood as she approached and pulled out his

chair. "Take my seat," he told her. "I need to get supplies."

She sat and scooted her chair to the table, but averted her eyes away from Mr. Ekola, sitting across.

"You can sure handle a spatula," Mr. Ekola said.

"I t-t-try," she said.

Feeling a slow burn on her cheeks, Hattie looked down at her grease-covered apron, and then remembered the hair net on her head. *I must look a fright.*

"Appreciate you helping. You're quite a gal," Mr. Ekola said. He pushed his chair back and stood.

Ivar walked over. "Girls, be at the wagon in an hour."

Mabs jumped up. "I need to get Teaspoon ready."

Bert looked at Eva and Tillie. "There are carrots and apples in the storeroom. Take a bucketful to your horse."

"G-g-go ahead," Hattie told them. "I'll help Bert with c-c-clean-up and I'll meet you at the wagon after."

While Hattie stood at the washtub scouring a fry pan, Bill and Tom scuttled in from the mess hall with tubs of dirty dishes, setting them at her feet. Hattie washed. Tom rinsed. Bill dried. Bert, at another washtub, scrubbed pots and pans. No one talked. When a steam whistle blasted one long blow, Bert stopped and listened. Six more long ones followed. Two short blasts after that. Bert wiped his hands on his apron and hightailed out the door, cursing.

Tom grimaced and shook his head. "The dreaded signal: seven long and two short blasts, means someone's hurt or dead."

CHAPTER NINE

HOURS LATER, Ivar staggered into the cookhouse and sat down at the table. His face showed fatigue. In silence, Bert poured two cups of coffee, walked over to the table, and set one of the cups in front of Ivar, then sat down beside him.

Ivar lifted his gaze to Bert. "John Mason."

"Sorry to hear," Bert said, his tone somber.

Hattie knew that she was witnessing an experience that the two had shared too many times before. She hung up her apron and tiptoed toward the door.

"Hattie," Ivar said. She paused and looked over her shoulder. "Please join us." She nodded and approached. "Where are the girls?" he asked.

Bert spoke up instead. "Pickin' blackberries."

"Good," said Ivar. "Not news for young girls' ears." He glanced at Hattie. She saw wetness in his eyes. "John was my father's oldest friend."

"I'm so s-s-sorry," she said.

"And a good man," Bert added.

"Yes," said Ivar, gazing into his coffee again. "My father must see John's wife, Pearl, right away and take him home." He looked up at Hattie. "I need to stay, but there's room on his wagon for three more. We should probably get the girls back to town, but...that means you'd be stuck here until the next supply wagon arrives. Should only be a week or so."

"Oh," she said, wringing her hands.

She wanted to be supportive, but wasn't sure how she felt being left behind. "M-m-maybe we should all wait. Seeing the body might f-f-frighten... the children."

Bert spoke up. "They won't see it. It's put into a wooden coffin. They'll think he's haulin' supplies."

Ivar sighed. "Tillie's such a talker and she'd lift my father's spirits, but I do understand your hesitation."

Bert looked at Hattie square on. "Awful hard trip for a man to make on his own. Company would be good."

"All right," said Hattie. "I'll get the g-g-girls ready now."

Hattie saw the wagon off and headed back to the cookhouse. "Any good at makin' pies?" Bert asked as she walked through the door.

"Yes." She didn't add that her pies had won first place at her hometown picnic.

"Blackberries and blueberries," he said. "Have at it."

While five pies cooled on the counter, Bert walked over and scooped a bite. "Flaky crust and perfect tartness," he said. "Bein' short-handed, I've only had time to make bread puddin'. It'll be a good treat on such a solemn day. I know the men will appreciate it."

"I'm g-g-glad to help."

"Need at least twelve more."

"Th-th-that's all?" she teased, but the truth was she enjoyed working in the cookhouse. It didn't require conversation. *If only the mercantile could be this easy.*

THE WEEK HAD settled into a workable routine. Hattie had even adjusted to the high-pitched whistles blasting throughout the day, but only after Bert snapped at her for being so jumpy. "You'll know the dreaded signal if it comes," he had told her. "It's seven long mournin' blows and two quick ones after that, not these short spurts we hear throughout the day." What Hattie found most interesting were the lumbermen themselves. Nearly all were bearded, burley, and hard-muscled, but when they traipsed out of camp with axes, mauls, and lunch pails they did so in an orderly gentlemen-like succession. Then there were those who'd walk single-file, twelve feet or so apart, with ten-foot saws balanced over their shoulders. With the teeth-blades facing out, the saws sprung up and down to the men's even pace.

That afternoon, rain battered the roof. "Do the men stop working when it's like this?" Hattie asked.

"Nope," said Bert. "They wear paraffin coats and tin pants."

"T-t-tin pants?"

"Canvas but look tin when they're wet," he remarked, "and stand straight up like half-legs when dryin' in a corner on their own."

"Huh," she said, trying to envision it.

"The men will be cold and extra hungry," Bert told her. "Roast beef, biscuits, mashed potatoes, and gravy usually does the trick. Plus, one of your tasty pies."

Right then, her brother Wallace popped into her head. Mother had always made him a similar dish on cold drizzly days. She turned when she heard the clickety-clack of buckboard wheels echoing through the opened door. A moment later, a middle-aged man rushed in.

"Howdy, Bert. Got any hot coffee?"

The bear-like man had a brown scraggly beard, round nose, and a friendly face. He removed his floppy hat, setting it on the table, and hung his buckskin coat over the back of an empty chair. Bert walked over with the coffeepot and two tin cups dangling from his fingers. After pouring the coffee, he sat opposite the man.

"Thank ye," the man said. "Got any eats?"

Bert hollered to Hattie, who was standing at the stove. "Hattie, please dish up a plate for Frank."

Hattie set the plate in front of the man. "This is Frank," Bert introduced and motioned for Hattie to sit down at the table, which she did. "Surprised to see you out in such sloppy weather," Bert said to Frank.

"Wagon was already loaded," Frank replied, "and I figured the rain would ease up. Guess I was wrong on that, but you won't be seeing anyone else for a while. The creek bridge washed out. I barely made it across."

"You don't say," Bert remarked.

"Hard to say when they'll get it fixed," Frank added.

"Lucky for us we got enough grub to last months."

Hattie's eyes widened. *Could I be stuck here that long?*

"THERE'S A SHINDY tonight," Bert later told her.

Hattie furrowed her brow. "What's that?"

"Music and dancin'."

"Dancing?"

"Yep," he said. "You'd think after six days of ten-hour shifts they'd want to rest, but not on Saturday nights.

The energetic ones are rarin' to go. Others play draw poker, jabber tall tales, or participate in arm-wrestlin'."

"I see," she said, now remembering the men playing poker when she and the girls arrived last Saturday and how the men hooted at her.

"I'm gettin' out of here before the hoopla starts," Bert said. "Suggest you do the same."

"I've got oatmeal c-c-cookies in the oven."

"You experimentin' again?"

"Yes, I added c-c-cinnamon and raisins."

Hattie liked whipping up different concoctions. It was her creative side, but she hadn't given any thought to it being Saturday night.

"See you in the mornin'," Bert told her, "and keep away from that door." He pointed to the doorway leading into the mess hall.

"Okay," she said. "G-g-goodnight, Bert."

A moment later, Ivar appeared. "Something smells good," he said, coming into the cookhouse at his usual six o'clock time. He preferred his meals in the cookhouse after the men had eaten. Hattie, Bert, and the flunkies finished their supper by four o'clock. He walked over to the cookstove and dished up a plate. There was always food left warming for any stragglers.

Leaning against the table, Ivar chewed and rested his eyes on Hattie. "The roast is tasty tonight."

"My mother's recipe," she admitted.

"What other talents do you have?"

"For you to f-f-find out, I suppose." She turned back to spooning batter onto the baking tray.

He slid along the table edge closer to her. "Am I being challenged? Or was that flirting?"

She felt his warm breath on her neck. Her knees almost buckled. Heat rose to her cheeks. "No, I-I-I...."

He saw that she was rattled, but was having too much fun to stop until banjo music drifted into the cookhouse. "The shindy," he said. "Forgot that was tonight. It will be a good diversion for the men." Hattie knew he was referring to John's accident earlier that week. "Let's join them and bring some cookies."

Hattie froze, uncertain what to say, then faced him. "I don't have a p-p-proper dress," she said, feeling foolish soon as she said it. She was wearing a brown-plaid frock that Bert had found in one of the flunky shacks. Surprisingly it fit. Tom, the cookhouse flunky, had said more than once how nice she looked in it.

Ivar stood back and measured every length of her with a devilish grin on his face. "You look fine to me."

As the banjos strummed, violins and harmonicas joined in, forcing a faster pace. Ivar set a large platter of cookies on the table and sat next to Hattie on the bench as she watched the lumberjacks moving to barn-dance steps.

"In and out with your partners, then an allemande...and a do-si-do," a caller repeated. Others clapped and stomped their feet. *"Swing your partner."*

Ivar leaned closer. "The men with handkerchiefs around their arms are the women," he told her.

"They're very g-g-good," noting some were expert steppers. "Have you ever done this?"

He nodded.

She wanted to ask what part he played, but decided not to. She was impressed that he admitted he danced with men.

Ivar reached for her hand. "Let's take a turn," bringing her with him to the middle of the floor.

"A real filly," a lumberjack shouted. "She's gotta be shared."

Hattie gulped.

"Suppose that is only fair," said Ivar.

Squeezing her hand tighter, Ivar swung Hattie back and forth to the called-out commands and handed her off to another man. It happened so fast, Hattie's head was spinning, her feet trying to keep in step. Another hand-off had her laughing so hard that it didn't matter who was holding her because in two more ins-and-outs, she was shuffled off again. By intermission, she was back with Ivar. He bowed and grabbed her hand, pulling her with him to the cookhouse, laughing most of the way. "You should've seen your face when you got passed from man to man," he chortled.

"V-v-very funny," she said, chuckling.

Laughing, he wiped cheerful tears off his cheek. "You are a good sport," he said. He grew serious. "You really are."

"I-I...," before she could finish with "I suppose," he wrapped his arms around her, pulled her close, and gently kissed her. Then his lips wandered to the curve of her neck, to her earlobe, and when his mouth met hers again, his warm lips seared jolts through her like nothing she'd ever felt before. Her lips responded with hungry passion, sending ripples through him and his chest hammering so hard that it scared him.

He released her and stumbled backwards. "What are we doing?" he said.

As if in shock, Hattie froze. "Wh-wh-what?" She blinked, trying to understand what he was asking.

"We're just friends," he insisted. "This was a mistake."

Heat rushed to her cheeks. Her head was now whirling in every direction, not knowing what to say or do. She cast her eyes downward to the floor.

"I'm sorry, Hattie. I truly am." And then he turned and headed toward the door.

CHAPTER TEN

BY MORNING, Hattie had collected her courage and walked into the cookhouse. *Act like nothing happened*, repeated in her head.

Hanging up her coat and grabbing an apron, she glanced over at the table where Ivar usually sat, but he wasn't there. She scanned the room, catching Bert's eye.

"If you're lookin' for Ivar," Bert said, "he packed up his breakfast and took off."

"Oh," Hattie said, trying to sound casual.

"Wasn't in the mood to converse," Bert added.

Feeling her face redden, she quickly tied the apron string around her back.

Bert gave her a puzzled look. "Somethin' happen between you two?"

"N-n-no."

"Good. 'Cuz later, you and I are headin' up to the steam donkeys with wash."

Suddenly her lip quivered. "Bert, I need a break." She didn't wait for his reply. She grabbed her coat and raced out the door. She headed to the clearing surrounded by blackberry bushes and sat on a fallen log. Tears cascaded down her cheeks.

All morning she had tried to put Ivar out of her head. *What a fool I am.* Josie had warned her that he might play games.

"What's causing tears to such a pretty face?" a voice said above her.

She wiped her cheeks with the back of her hand and jerked her head up to a handsome, dark-haired logger. He was clean-shaven, square-jawed, and dressed in a green plaid shirt, canvas pants, and boots. His legs were long and his body muscular.

He crouched down beside her. He had seen her in the cookhouse, but hadn't realized how pretty she was until now. His smile broadened. "I'm Nick Cooper."

Hattie felt her face redden. "H-H-Hattie."

"Would you like to talk about it?"

"It's nothing," she reassured, pasting on a smile. She turned her head away. "I n-n-need to go." She gathered her skirt, and just as she started to stand up, he offered her his hand. Hattie grasped on to it, steadied up to her feet, but bounced into his chest.

"I've seen you in the cookhouse." He refrained from saying more, fearing it might scare her off.

"I don't recall s-s-seeing you." She was surprised that she hadn't noticed him. Most of the men were scruffy and older. Nick was handsome and young. She guessed him to be in his mid-twenties.

"Just got back from cleaning up," he told her. "I had a beard, like every other man here."

The last thing that Hattie wanted was involvement with another man. Even as a friend. "Appreciate your c-c-concern," she said, "but I need to get b-b-back."

"Unless you want others asking questions, I'd advise you wait until the wetness leaves your eyes."

Hattie sighed, then nodded, still feeling the sting of Ivar's rejected kiss.

"I can leave you to yourself," Nick offered, "or give you a lesson on birds."

"Birds?"

"Sure," he said. "All types in these woods. Just the other day I was getting ready to fell a tree when I spotted three baby woodpeckers in a nearby alder. I had to realign my cut so I wouldn't destroy their nest."

"You're a faller?"

Bert had told her that fallers had one of the most dangerous jobs in the woods. They were the cutters of the giant trees and had to be careful of widowmakers—heavy branches shaken loose by the faller that could fall without warning and flatten him dead.

"Yes, I'm a faller," he said. "I could balance on a springboard at fourteen and handle axes and saws as good as my pa."

A springboard was a tapered wooden plank that was placed into slots cut into the butt of a tree.

"It's good quick money. Allows me to move on."

Hattie had also heard that most fallers were drifters.

"Back to the woodpeckers," he said. "There's quite a variety: the red-breasted sapsucker, the red-crested, and the flickers. There's a white-headed one too."

"I've never s-s-seen any up close, but I enjoy listening to their t-t-tapping." She smiled up at him. "I'm feeling b-b-better now. Nice to meet you."

"Same here."

"ARE YOU ALL RIGHT?" Bert asked Hattie as she walked through the cookhouse door.

Just needed air," she said. "I'm ready to h-h-help with the wash."

Bert pointed to a basket. "Grab that one and I'll get this other. We'll pick up your garments on the way."

At the perimeter of the camp, old oil drums filled with water were heating over a fire for the men to retrieve hot water for their wash. Hattie watched in amazement as the lumberjacks threw soap powder and lye into their tubs, tossed in their clothes, and plunged up and down with a long-handled device, making suds as they washed.

"Looks like they're churning b-b-butter," said Hattie.

"Same principal," Bert remarked.

"Never knew lumberjacks liked to be...so clean."

"Not all of 'em. Some smell worse than skunks. And don't get me started on those who chew snoose."

Hattie learned all about Copenhagen, the chewing tobacco—snoose—after she had stepped into a patch. Bert told her that the men would go on strike if they didn't have it to chew. He always kept a six-month supply on hand.

"What about those early morning d-d-donkey punchers?" she asked. "I d-d-don't see any of them down here w-w-washing."

"They're the kings of the camp," Bert said. "Every Sunday they earn extra pay for maintenance, whether the donkeys need it or not, and have access to scaldin' water from the boilers. Some fill washtubs for weekly baths."

"Goodness me," Hattie said, hoping she wouldn't encounter any of the men bathing. She wondered if that was where Nick had cleaned up.

"Maybe we can get Ivar to draw you a bath."

Hattie's eyes widened. "Ivar?"

"Yep, he's one that likes to be clean and shaven."

Her stomach fluttered. *Why did I come?*

"I take advantage bathin' at least once a month," Bert added. "It's all private, behind the shed."

"Not for me," Hattie said.

Nearing the ridge, Hattie spotted three steam-donkeys. Ivar had drawn a picture of one.

"They're spurtin' good," Bert said, looking at the white smoke spewing from the tall stacks. "Those iron oxen should be givin' us lots of hot water today."

"Oxen?" said Hattie.

"The machines work the same as the animal—haulin' logs from the woods, riggin' the trees, and pullin' loads. It's back breakin' work without 'em, but smaller camps still do it all with only men, skids, and animals," he added. "I believe I see Ivar up ahead."

Turning bright red, she sheepishly glanced at Bert and stopped mid-step. "I think I should go back."

Bert shook his head. "Nothin' goin' on with you two, eh? You've been actin' odd all morning and he was too." Bert pointed to a fallen log. "Take a seat. Be right back."

Hattie watched as Bert stomped toward Ivar. They were out of earshot, but she could tell by Bert's flapping arms that he was giving Ivar an earful. Her stomach tied into knots. Her emotions were already jumbled and she didn't need Bert piling on more.

"What's goin' on between you and the girl?" Bert asked Ivar. "You've been flirtin' with her all week. And now, the both of you mouth-clamped, walkin' on eggs."

Ivar sighed. "We had a bit of a misunderstanding."

"Go fix it," Bert barked, inching closer to Ivar. "Don't need a sulkin' girl in my cookhouse."

"It's not that simple," Ivar said, shifting back and forth. "I accidently kissed her then took it back."

Bert scowled at him. "Can't take somethin' like that back. You either smooched or you didn't."

Ivar shrugged.

"So you think you're too good fer the girl?"

"No," Ivar insisted, not wanting to admit that he had feelings for Hattie. Kissing her was all he had thought about that whole evening at the shindy.

"Then what is it?"

"I'm a college man and have a set plan and don't want to be detoured."

"And you think she'd do that?"

"Not on purpose."

"I'll tell you this. She's a nice gal and you'd be lucky to snag her, but now she's got hurt feelins'." Bert stabbed his finger at Ivar. "Get over there and smooth it out."

IVAR APPROACHED and caught Hattie's glance. He took a deep breath and sat beside her. "Bert's right...we need to get this kiss behind us."

She abruptly turned toward him. "You t-t-told him?"

"He knew something was going on."

She clasped her hands and looked down at her lap. "I'm v-v-very embarrassed." Mother's words raced through her head. *Men don't desire stuttering girls.*

"I'm sorry to have caused that," he said. "Please forgive me. Can't we just be friends?" His gut clenched. It was taking his full restraint not to take her into his arms. He saw hurt in her eyes and wanted to comfort her. "I got caught up in the moment," he added.

"So d-d-did I," Hattie admitted. The evening had overwhelmed her emotions, but her feelings for him still lingered and she wasn't sure how to unravel those.

"That's it then," he said. "No more music for us." His kidding eased the tension.

"Y-y-yes."

"Good." He jumped up and grabbed her arm, pulling her to her feet. He picked up her wash basket and looped her arm through his. "Let's get this wash started," he said, walking her toward Bert.

Hattie guessed that he had taken a bath. He was clean-shaven and his blond hair in place. When he caught her gaze, she looked away.

"Everything's fine," Ivar told Bert. He turned back to Hattie. "I'll do your wash and draw you a bath."

"No," said Hattie.

"Please," he said. "Accept it as my token of friendship."

She gasped and looked at Bert.

"I wouldn't be refusin'," Bert said. "A bath's a real treat. But get goin' if yer gonna do it and don't dawdle. I plan on soakin' in the tub after you."

CHAPTER ELEVEN

THE NEXT WEEK the rain never ceased, but most of her awkwardness around Ivar had. How much more embarrassing could it get? They shared a kiss and then he fixed her a bath. And it was wonderful to be clean and to have a clean dress. "Makes you better friends when you share a muddle," Bert had told her. She decided he was right.

"When d-d-do you think I'll be able to get back to town?" she asked Bert.

He gave her a sympathetic stare. "You goin' stir crazy?"

"N-n-no, but my help is needed by my family."

"Imagine so. Once this rain lets up, a crew will rebuild the bridge. Shouldn't take but a couple days. Be sorry to see you go."

Hattie nodded, ready to tell him the same until she heard the long slow whistle mourning through the camp. Even though Bert acted unconcerned, his eyes revealed differently. It sparked fear in Hattie too. She knew some of the lumberjacks by name and she had an attachment. Nick, for one, popped into her head.

"Probably just a signal to move a log," Bert told her. "Time's a wastin'. I'll be in the stockroom. Holler if you need me."

Washing carrots for the stew, she didn't hear the footsteps until a thunderous voice called out, "Need help."

She spun around and gasped when she saw Ivar slumped between two men, supported under their shoulders. She rubbed her wet hands on her apron and called out, "B-B-Bert...B-B-Bert."

"What is it?" he said, rushing out of the stockroom. "Ivar's b-b-been hurt."

Without hesitation, Bert raced over and swiped his hand across the table, pushing utensils to the floor. "Put him here," he told the men. "What happened?"

"Cable snapped and grazed him in the head," one of the men said. "He's dazed and losing blood."

Hattie yanked off her apron and handed it to Bert. "Use th-th-this for the blood. I'll get water." She filled a bucket and carried it over, setting it down at Bert's feet.

"Get bandages, gauze, and rags," Bert told her, "second shelf in the stockroom." He looked at the lumberjacks. "We'll take it from here. Thanks for what you did."

Hattie hurried back with an armful of supplies. Bert grabbed a wash rag from her, dunked it in water, and patted Ivar's head. Within seconds, it was saturated with blood. "He needs stitches and whiskey," Bert said, dropping the blood-soaked rag on the floor. "Wet some gauze," he told Hattie. "Put it on the wound and keep pressure on it until I get back."

FOR THE NEXT five days, Ivar needed constant care and was confined to Mr. Ekola's living quarters—a separate room attached to the office. It housed a potbellied stove, two sitting chairs, and two single beds on opposite walls. Hattie agreed to be the full-time caretaker. Under Bert's direction, the flunkies, Bill and Tom, hung a rope in the middle of the room and draped it with a sheet, giving Hattie privacy while she slept. During the day, Bert spelled her whenever he could.

That night, a sharp noise startled Hattie awake. She jumped out of bed, grabbed her lantern still lit, and raced over to Ivar. She saw that he had knocked his tin cup onto the floor. She picked it up. Ivar clutched onto her arm.

"Who are you?" he said in a frightened tone. Bert had warned her that Ivar might show confusion.

She lifted the lantern closer to her face and leaned down. "It's me, H-H-Hattie." She hoped her stuttering wouldn't confuse him more, but from the puzzlement on his face, she realized that it did. "I'm your... nurse." She felt odd misleading him, but Bert had instructed to keep explanations simple, "and fib if you have to."

After Ivar closed his eyes again, Hattie sat beside his bed and rewetted a cloth, placing it on his forehead. She repeated the steps until she fell asleep in the chair. Hours later, she awoke to Ivar gently squeezing her hand.

Her eyes fluttered open and her stomach stirred as she saw him studying her face.

He tightened his grip. "Why am I in this bed with you sitting here?"

"You h-h-hurt...your head," she told him. He felt his forehead. "And you need to keep still."

"What day is it?" he asked.

"Tuesday. You've been d-d-down for five days."

He grimaced. "I'd like to get up." He shimmied to the edge of the bed, then slowly swung his legs over and dangled them along the side. He took a deep breath, pushed into the mattress, and stood. When he wobbled, Hattie seized his arm and steadied him backwards onto the bed.

"It's too soon," she insisted.

"Seems you're right," said Ivar.

WITH IVAR'S improvement, some of Hattie's normalcy returned. For one, she was sleeping in her own flunky shack and spending more time in the cookhouse. Bert's helpers, Bill and Tom, were now watching after Ivar at night.

"I'll visit with Ivar this evening," Bert told Hattie. "Try to get some rest." But resting to Hattie never included sitting. Instead, she started on buttermilk biscuits for breakfast.

She carried the first batch out to the mess hall for the men playing cards. When she turned to head back to the cookhouse, she spotted Nick Cooper, the handsome dark-haired logger, with a book in hand sitting on the floor, his upper back leaning against the wall. He was so engrossed reading that he never looked up. She didn't realize that she was staring at him until one of the card-playing men said, "What you looking at over there, missy?"

Nick glanced up.

Hattie quickly looked away. She hurried to the cookhouse. *Did he see me? What must he think?* After a bit, she had settled down and mindlessly started on another batch of biscuits.

No sooner had she closed the oven door that she was startled by a deep voice. She swung around, bumped her elbow into the empty platter in his hands, and knocked it to the floor. Staring into Nick's brown eyes, heat rose to her cheeks.

"Sorry, didn't mean to frighten you," he said, retrieving the platter and setting it in the washtub. With his backside against the table, he crossed his arms and studied her face. *What a pretty girl.* He cleared his throat. "Came to tell you how good your biscuits were. Have you worked here long?"

"No, just a short while. It's...only...t-t-temporary, but I like helping Bert."

He nodded. "How did you end up here?" He was hoping her answer wasn't that she was courting a logger or worse, engaged or married.

"Got stranded," she admitted, giving him a summary: a broken wagon wheel, her nieces heading back to town, and the road washing out.

"What bad luck," he said. A smile crossed his face, "but I must admit that it's nice to talk to someone who doesn't look like a grizzly bear." He pointed to a stray curl falling across her eye. "May I fix that for you?" Her hands were covered in flour and she had tried to push the loose strand away with the back of her wrist. He leaned toward her and gently tucked it behind her ear.

Her heart galloped like a runaway horse. "Would you like another b-b-biscuit?" she asked.

"Sure, if you can spare one."

Hattie motioned to five trays and then noticed a book propped under his arm. "W-w-what are you reading?"

"Edgar Allen Poe," he said, reaching for a biscuit. "Helps me sleep."

"Poe? His w-w-words are so haunting."

"Many find his writing dark," Nick said, "but I search for the hidden meaning. Most poems have one."

"Really? I recall most of his writings ending with d-d-death."

"It's more than that," he said. "Loss of love. Poe is one of my favorites. Must seem odd to you for a logger to enjoy poetry."

"Yes...but nice."

"My strong-natured mother insisted that my brothers and I learn the arts. It stuck with me." He looked at the washtub filled with greasy pans. "How about I help you clean up, then I'll recite you a poem."

Before she could answer, he rolled up his shirtsleeves, exposing his muscular arms, and walked to the washtub. Reaching for a brush, he started scrubbing a pan and glanced at her. "Are you just going to stand there and let me do all the work?" he teased.

"N-n-no," she said, turning back to the biscuits, covering them with a cloth. She wiped the flour off her hands with a wet rag. "I'm done," she announced.

"I am too." He followed Hattie to the table and sat across from her. He focused on her face. "*The Raven*," he read.

Hattie interjected. "*Once upon a midnight dreary.*"

He grinned and leaned back in his chair. "You know it."

"I do. My m-m-mother was a schoolteacher. I'm well-versed, but that poem always s-s-scared me."

"Then, nevermore," he said.

Hattie smirked, knowing that *nevermore* was the final line of *The Raven*.

He thumbed through his book. "How do you feel about *Annabel Lee*?"

"I only remember parts," said Hattie.

"I don't know it all to memory either. I'll read it."

She studied every line of his face: his square jaw, small dimple at the corner of his mouth, twitching as he read. And those piercing brown eyes. Every time he glanced up at her, she melted.

"*Of my darling—my darling—my life and my bride. In her sepulcher there by the sea.*" His voice faded, "*In her tomb by the sounding sea.*"

"A sep-ull-ker?" Hattie asked. "Isn't that a rock m-m-monument ...for a d-d-dead person?"

He broke out into laughter, his eyes twinkling as he looked at her. "Yes."

She grinned. "I'm t-t-teasing you. It was beautiful."

He nodded. "I hope someday to find a love as deep."

Not sure how to respond, Hattie froze, awestruck. She had never met anyone like him.

He stood. "Don't know about you, but if I don't get going, I'll be too tired to sleep."

Escorting her to her flunky shack, Nick cupped his hand on her elbow and held the lantern with his other. "Poetry captures my soul," he told her. "Do you feel that way about anything?"

"No, I've been a d-d-dairy…maid most of m-m-my life. Milking c-c-cows, churning butter, working the farm. There's things I'm g-g-good at and like to do, but n-n-nothing that's caught my passion. I envy you."

When they reached her cabin, his heart raced, but he fought the urge to kiss her. He quickly released his hand from her elbow. "Parting from you is such sweet sorrow. Until we meet again, my lady." He reached for her hand and gently kissed it, and then he backed away while still looking at her.

Butterflies flittered in her stomach and she went weak-kneed. "Who are you r-r-reciting now?"

"A little Shakespeare mixed with Robin Hood," he answered, then winked.

"Are you t-t-taking me to Nottingham or Sherwood Forest tomorrow?" she asked kiddingly.

"Perhaps I am."

For a week, Nick read her poetry. One night, he talked about his life. She learned that he had just returned from working five months on a Wyoming cattle ranch. He had read a book about one and decided he wanted to try it, but not great money and harder work than he thought.

"Harder than being a f-f-faller?" asked Hattie.

"Not as dangerous, but riding a horse and roping a cow can be as physical."

"So, you r-r-read an adventure and then head off to t-t-try it?"

"Yep," he said. "I've worked in silver mine, on a paddleboat on the Mississippi, and a steamship sailing from San Francisco to New York City."

"What an exciting l-l-life."

"It has been," he said, "but I'm ready for a rest."

"I noticed your r-r-ring, such a pretty stone," said Hattie, "but you don't w-w-wear it at work, do you?"

"No, I find good hiding spots. It's jade." He took it off and handed it to Hattie. "A nine-year-old girl named Becca gave it to me. A prospector gave it to her. She was special, the type that touches your soul."

Hattie rotated the band in her palm. "So, you had it made into a r-r-ring to remember her?" He nodded. "It's lovely," said Hattie. "Why did she g-g-give it to you?"

"Five years ago, I got the itch to go to the Klondike to dig for gold."

"The Alaskan Gold Rush," Hattie affirmed.

"Yep. I had just turned nineteen and it was my first adventure. Before that, I was felling trees in Oregon with my father and brothers.

Hattie listened intently as he told her about Becca Slater, the nine-year-old girl who had given him the stone. Her parents had been Kansas farmers, but their last harvest barely put food on the table, so they sold their farm and used the money for Alaska. There were three kids: two older boys and Becca. Money went fast. They didn't know until they reached Skagway that the Klondike was in Canada and anyone crossing had to have one year's worth of supplies.

Hattie shook her head and sighed.

"After weeks on White Pass, the father sized it up and realized they'd made a mistake," said Nick. "Others who had made the journey and were heading back hollered to those still coming, "*Turn around, nothing left. Only the merchants and saloon owners getting rich.*"

"I read about that," said Hattie.

"When the Slater family arrived back to Seattle, they were penniless. I met them in a soup kitchen."

"How t-t-terrible for them," said Hattie.

Nick nodded. "I cancelled my trip passage and bought them train tickets back to Kansas. Mr. Slater still had a brother there. I gave them extra spending money too. Becca was so grateful that she gave me the stone. She was the sweetest angel, the kind of little girl that I hope to have one day."

Hattie was so stirred by this story that tears started pooling in her eyes.

Nick looked at her quizzically. "Are you all right?"

"What a k-k-kind man you are, and you're only twenty-four," she said, shaking her head.

He gently touched her hand. "Hattie, I think you would've done the same. Bet Bert would have too."

CHAPTER TWELVE

"W*HERE ARE YOU GOING*?" was Ivar's constant question to Hattie. Midday, Bert walked in with the coffeepot. Hattie leaped to her feet. She was stiff from sitting. She wouldn't be seeing Nick tonight. He and a crew were felling trees up on the ridge and would be camping out for the next few days. Hattie packed their meals, added pies and a special tart for Nick.

"Take your time," Bert told her.

When Ivar opened his eyes and sat up, he quickly scanned the room. "Where's Hattie?"

"Gone," Bert said. "Want some coffee?"

"Sure," said Ivar. He looked at Bert. "Hattie's been acting odd lately. Any idea why?"

Bert chuckled under his breath and scratched his chin. "Come to think of it, a strapin' good-lookin' fella with dark hair has been stoppin' by. Asked fer extra fixins', but spends most his time feastin' eyes on Hattie. He's been by all week."

Ivar's jaw stiffened. "A logger?"

"He's a faller," said Bert. "Don't see what it hurts."

"You can't be serious," said Ivar. "Fallers are cocky. Most are drifters. He's probably got a girl in every town."

"Just 'cause Hattie stutters don't mean she doesn't have good sense," said Bert. "I keep a watchful eye. Only thing that might be happenin' is he plants a kiss on those pretty lips." When Ivar squirmed, Bert couldn't resist a final jab. "And I guarantee *he* won't be takin' it back."

Ivar scowled. "Nice poke, Bert, but I care about Hattie and you're just making a joke of it all."

"Suppose that's true," he admitted, "but for someone who only wants to be friends with the girl, you're sure showin' jagged fangs."

Bert entered the cookhouse chuckling.

Hattie turned. "What's so funny?"

"A private joke. What are you doin'?"

"M-m-making a dessert tray for Ivar."

"You sure take good care of that boy."

"He's a good friend," she said.

Bert chortled. "That friend wasn't too happy to hear about that other young feller comin' around."

"Ivar knows about that?"

"He's aware."

"Shouldn't m-m-matter," said Hattie. "Ivar thinks of m-m-me as a sister."

"Uh, huh. Well if that's the case, are you considerin' givin' this other young fella a chance?"

"N-n-no...he'll be moving on and so will I."

"Sometimes love blossoms in strange places."

"But I st-st-stutter."

"I'm guessin' he already picked up on that." Bert gave her a serious look. "Hattie, have you looked at yourself in the mirror lately?"

"Y-y-yes, of course."

"But probably *not* like a man would view you. You're a striking young woman, curves in the right places too."

Hattie gasped. "B-B-Bert."

"Don't give me that. I'm not flirtin', just givin' you facts. Don't think Ivar hasn't noticed either."

She grabbed the tray. "I b-b-better get back to him."

When Hattie walked through the door, Ivar was still fuming over Bert's remarks and he tried to conceal it.

She placed the tray down and quickly sat, rattled from her own conversation with Bert. "Wh-wh-what are you reading?" referring to a magazine in his lap.

"Logging stories," Ivar said. "My dad has a stack. We also have a bookshelf in the mess hall filled with more. I can't get past the first page without my head throbbing."

"W-w-want me to r-r-read it to you?"

Ivar paused. *How embarrassing might that be for her if she stutters?* He spoke fast. "No, that's all right."

She ignored him, reached for the magazine, and flipped to the first page. "*I remember as if it were yesterday, trees the width of a sailing ship.*"

Ivar interrupted. "You're not stuttering."

"Not when I r-r-read or sing or do tongue twisters."

"Has it always been that way?"

"Yes, soon as I started t-t-talking. My teacher called it dys...flu...ency where my brain gives too much thought...to my words."

"Maybe it can be cured."

She shrugged and said, "No."

He nodded, then reached for Hattie's hand. "Bert mentioned that a faller has been stopping by the cookhouse. Is he bothering you?"

"No. He's v-v-very nice. Last night we had tea while he told...stories."

Ivar narrowed his eyes. "Last night?"

"When Bert spelled me so I could bake."

Ivar gritted his teeth and released her hand. "You were alone with him?" Her hesitation infuriated him. "Fallers are trouble. You need to stay away from him."

"N-n-nothing happened."

"Stop being so naïve," he said, anger seething in his voice. "He could be a scoundrel for all you know, frequenting the brothels and drinking."

Ivar's attitude surprised her. For a brief moment, she thought that he might be jealous.

Ivar creased his brow. He wanted to believe her, but his gut wasn't sure. He checked his emotions before he spoke. "I don't want you getting hurt."

Averting his stare, she flipped through the magazine. "We're just friends." She didn't add that she couldn't wait to see Nick again. "He's b-b-been a gentleman."

Ivar's jaw clamped tight and an overwhelming possessiveness overtook him. *If you don't tell him to leave you alone, I will.* He sighed under his breath. *Why can't I tell her how I feel?* Much as Ivar didn't want to admit it, he was torn by her stuttering. Part of him thought he had accepted it. He sure cared enough about her to want to, but then self-doubt crept in. How would he react if she stuttered around his college friends? Would he be embarrassed? He hoped he was better than that. He reached for her hand again. "Hattie, will you please not see him anymore? Please, do it for me."

Before she could answer, a woman's voice called out, "IVAR!"

Ivar's mouth flew open, so did Hattie's. Hattie quickly slid her hand out of Ivar's and stepped back.

Mrs. Ekola, with Josie and Mr. Ekola behind her, rushed into the room to Ivar's bed. Mrs. Ekola kissed his forehead then burst into sobs. "I can't do this again," his mother spouted. "I already lost one son to this camp." She cast her eyes to her husband. "He's *never* to come here again."

"Yes, dear," is all his father said.

Ivar's dumbfounded gaze caught Hattie's, but his attention shifted to Josie when she placed her finger under his chin and fluttered her long lashes, drawing his eyes to hers. She leaned down, lingered her lips on his, and whispered, "I'll be at your side until you're well."

A pit gnawed in Hattie's stomach. She glanced at Ivar's parents, but neither one of them seemed fazed by Josie's open affection. Ivar appeared transfixed.

Mr. Ekola broke the spell. "We would've been here sooner, son, if we'd known," his father's voice cracking. "Frank just hit town last night to give us the news. We got the wagon loaded and headed out early this morning."

Ivar looked at his father. "The road's reopened?"

"No. I paid Frank extra to bring us the back way."

"That must've taken at least five hours," said Ivar.

"It was a long trip," his mother added, "but we're so glad that we did it. I fretted the entire way." Placing a hankie to her face, she quivered and broke into sobs again.

"No need to cry, Mother," he said, trying to console her. "I'm almost healed, thanks to..." He peered around

Josie to capture Hattie's gaze again. "Nurse Hattie." Hattie, now next to the door, was close to escape, but froze when she heard her name.

"Hattie?" Josie said, moving her head to look. Her surprised expression revealed that she hadn't noticed Hattie in the room.

"Yes," he said. "At first, I needed day and night care, so she slept in the second bed." He pointed.

Hattie gulped. *Why'd he have to offer that?* She glanced at Ivar, but caught Josie's stare, cold as steel boring through her.

Mr. Ekola walked over and clasped Hattie's hand. "So glad you were here," he told her. "I'm sure you took excellent care of our boy."

Hattie blushed, heat now rushing to her ears and neck as well. "I'll l-l-leave you to visit," she said. Spinning around on her heels, she double-stepped out of the room.

MR. EKOLA WALKED into the cookhouse, sat down at the table with Hattie and Bert, and looked at Hattie. "Came to tell you the wagon's leaving early. About seven a.m. You'll need to be ready. I'm staying here at the camp. Frank will be driving all of you back to town."

"Oh," said Hattie, her stomach churning. She dreaded being stuck with Mrs. Ekola and Josie on such a long ride back. "M-m-maybe I should s-s-stay another week to give more room in the wagon."

Bert shook his head. "Much as I'd love to have you longer, it's time for you to go."

"Bert's right," Mr. Ekola added. "It could be another two weeks before Frank makes it back here."

Hattie nodded.

"I have some good news," he continued. "The Missus and Josie already settled into their own flunky shack, so won't be sharing with you tonight."

EARLY MORNING, Bert's frequent glances made Hattie misty-eyed. "Gonna miss you, girl," he repeated for the third time. Hattie had given Bert her Wisconsin address and the Hoquiam store one too, insisting that they keep in touch. She gave Bert a note for Nick.

She patted her heart. "I'll miss you, Bert."

"Me too," he said.

Mr. Ekola walked in. "Ivar's being loaded now."

Hattie nodded and pulled her apron off and hung it on the hook. When she turned, Bert was at her side.

"Not walkin' you out," Bert said. "Got enough emotions stirrin.'" As he wrapped his arms around her, Hattie realized that she might never see him again and started to cry, but swallowed back her tears. He released her and glanced away from her gaze. "No more goodbyes," he said hoarsely. "Get goin'." He quickly strode over to the stove.

Tom stepped over. "It was fun working with you."

"I'll miss you and Bill." She really meant it. Tom and Bill, both skinny freckle-faced boys, had become substitute brothers. She hugged Tom. "Tell B-B-Bill I said good-bye." She raced out the door, tears streaming down her cheeks.

Reaching the wagon, she saw Ivar bedded in the back with Josie sitting close to him. Mr. Ekola meandered over, pulling on his chin. "You'll be riding on the springboard next to Mrs. Ekola." He helped Hattie up to the wagon, and then he tilted his face up to his wife. "Greta, be kind to this young girl."

"Of course, I will," she asserted, patting Hattie's hand. "I'll try to spare you from talking much."

Even though Mrs. Ekola's gesture was meant in kindness, it made Hattie self-conscious. Hattie pasted on a smile, a routine she'd learned since childhood. Suddenly, Mother popped into her head. "Consider it compassion when others try to shield you," her mother often told her, but Hattie thought they were trying to shield their own awkwardness, not hers.

Hattie looked back at the cookhouse and spotted Bert and Tom at the doorway. They waved and she frantically waved back until the wagon pulled away.

CHAPTER THIRTEEN

THE SECOND DAY back from the camp, Hattie grew restless. She headed to Daphanie's first, only to find that she was in Oregon staying with a cousin. Next, she visited with Mr. Connell until a customer interrupted. She had debated about seeing Ivar. Initially, she had decided no, but softened and headed to his house. Reaching their walkway, she paused. *Maybe this is a mistake. No, we are friends. It's important I see him.*

Mrs. Ekola greeted Hattie at the front door. "Let's sit on the porch swing," she said, motioning Hattie to it. Once seated, Mrs. Ekola faced her. "You were such a dear how you cared for our Ivar, but now it's up to his family. I'm sure you understand." Hattie nodded. "And you must think of Josie too. I'm asking that you stay away and let them blossom as a couple, like any good aunt would do."

"Yes," said Hattie, scolding herself under her breath for coming. She stood. "P-p-please give him my best."

"Of course, dear."

The closer Hattie got to the store, the more her anxiety grew. She so enjoyed working with Bert and didn't relish the idea of spending mornings with Mrs. Bailey again. Hattie took a deep breath and walked through the door.

"Hattie," Mrs. Bailey said excitedly. "Thank goodness you're back."

Stunned, Hattie braced for one of Mrs. Bailey's rude remarks. "Is s-s-something wrong?"

"I'm overwhelmed," she said, blowing out an exasperated sigh. "Governor McBride and his wife are visiting Grays Harbor. The Ladies Club is planning a reception and a formal ball in their honor."

"Oh... s-s-sounds like wonderful news."

"I should say so," she said, pursing her lips. "The Veysey Mercantile is the only store in the county that can handle such an up-scale event."

Hattie stood patiently as Mrs. Bailey droned on. She learned that the planning committee was stopping by shortly to pick out dresses and hats. And that Hattie's brother Charles and his new wife Nettie were now in Chicago, selecting gowns scheduled to arrive to the store by the end of this week. They were then traveling to San Francisco to choose more.

MRS. CUSHMAN and Mrs. Wiggins walked into the store with several others. Hattie stood at the shelves dusting, but caught their glances more than once. Even though she had mentally prepared for their arrival, seeing them again unraveled her far more than she had expected. *Wish I was back at the logging camp.*

One of the women stopped. "I'm Mrs. Tuttle," she said, greeting Hattie with a friendly smile.

No taller than five feet, the petite woman had wiry-brown hair piled atop her head like a bird's nest, which added at least two inches to her height.

"H-h-hello."

Mrs. Cushman looked over her shoulder at Mrs. Tuttle. "Lois, we have business to tend to."

Mrs. Tuttle winked. "A stuffy bunch, aren't they?"

Hattie gulped, squelching a giggle, and followed the women to the back counter where Hattie had set out *Montgomery Ward Catalogs* and other fashion books too. Mrs. Bailey had instructed Hattie to keep close.

The women thumbed through the catalogs, marking selections. Mrs. Cushman instructed, "Those who live along the river will wear blue hats, the country women, green. Townspeople, yellow, and the ones up on the hill, pink." She turned to Mrs. Bailey. "We'll need this order placed by Friday and I expect you to handle it personally. It's far too important to give to simple minds."

Hattie knew Mrs. Cushman was referring to her and wanted to say, don't worry, I have no intention of getting involved.

"You have my assurance," said Mrs. Bailey.

"Ladies," Mrs. Cushman continued, "since we are the committee heads, our hats must be the most ornate."

Mrs. Bailey looked at Hattie. "Get the San Francisco catalogs."

Hattie quickly retrieved the heavy books and set them down on the long counter. Mrs. Bailey gave her a quick nod. "Wait in the stockroom. I'll call if I need you."

At the end of the week, Mrs. Bailey rushed into the store waving the newspaper. "Come see."

Hattie, at a clothing rack straightening blouses, walked over to the front counter where Mrs. Bailey had spread out the newspaper. "It's nice," she said, impressed by how professional the advertisement looked.

Figure 7
(Courtesy of Veysey Family Collection)

With the advertisements in the papers and Charles' Chicago shipment displayed, the store grew into a circus of shoppers—some ordering from the catalogs, others pulling off garments the instant they were hung up, and the line-up for the fitting rooms a carnival of itself. Mrs. Bailey hired her sister-in-law and a cousin to assist. Hattie tended to the shelves and the racks.

"Hattie," Mrs. Bailey's voice shrilled. "Saturday will be our busiest day. You'll need to work the back counter."

"B-b-but."

"And control that stuttering. Perhaps Eva and Tillie can help with the talking. Josie is assisting with the catalogs. Mabs will be making deliveries. Make yourself presentable and get prepared for tomorrow."

The rest of the afternoon, Hattie fretted. She was relieved when Eva and Tillie agreed to help her.

"What if you read to the customers?" Eva asked. "You don't stutter when you read to us."

Hattie stared at the girls. "I n-n-never thought to use notes. Help me w-w-write out some. If I get into trouble, you can hand me one...to read aloud."

"And singing," Tillie said. "I've heard you at church and you don't stutter there."

Hattie laughed. "C-c-can you imagine the looks?"

The next morning before Mrs. Bailey unlocked the double front doors, she scanned the store for a final inspection.

Mannequins in the windows and throughout the store displayed multiple styles: ruffles, flouncy skirts, and simple A-line silhouettes, to name a few. Rows of satin shoes and boots lined the shelves, and petticoats and hankies were nicely placed on the wooden tables. Front and center were the Chicago and San Francisco ball gowns of various shades.

Hattie surveyed the store in disbelief and determined that it looked as fine as a New York one shown in the *McCall's Magazine*. She, Josie, and Mrs. Bailey had worked well into the night, surprisingly without any squabbles. Hattie's absence from visiting Ivar seemed to smooth out Josie's mood toward her, even more so after Hattie said, "Too many visitors will wear him out, so it should be only you."

Mrs. Bailey headed to the front doors, and then turned around to the workers. "Ready, girls?"

"Yes," several shouted.

The doors flew open. Women rushed to the racks, some pulling off two or three dresses until Mrs. Bailey got involved. "Ladies, please," Mrs. Bailey pleaded, "one outfit to a customer. We'll make a list for each dress and the interested party can add their name to try it on until it's sold." She motioned to her sister-in-law. "Bring a pencil and paper."

Josie stayed clear of it all and stood behind the catalog counter, dealing with those who wanted special orders. Mrs. Bailey's cousin was at the main counter for the final sales. Hattie and her young nieces waited at the back for any overflow. Hattie prayed they'd never be summoned, but that wish was quickly erased.

"Hattie," Mrs. Bailey called out. She pointed to two women fighting over a blue dress. "Handle that."

Hattie walked over to the clothing rack, hoping that the two women might resolve the situation on their own. "W-w-what's...the issue?"

"I saw it first," a chubby woman said.

"It's too small for her," the thinner younger one remarked, trying to pull the dress out of the heavier woman's hands.

Hattie faced the over-sized shopper. "That blue one...won't f-f-fit you. Perhaps...."

"How dare you," the large woman blurted.

Mrs. Bailey scurried over and corralled the irritated customer, bringing her to Josie's counter and making gestures toward Hattie as she talked. Hattie wondered what disparaging remark she was making about her.

Josie acknowledged the woman immediately and flipped through the catalog. As Hattie watched Josie—so confident and calm with a reassuring smile—her stomach twanged with envy. When another tussle erupted, Hattie wandered over. She hoped that this incident wasn't as unnerving as the last one. "M-m-may I help you?"

"That girl has on the dress that was hung up for me," an older woman said. "Why wasn't it guarded?"

"I-I-I..." She quickly closed her mouth, frustrated.

The older woman, waiting for Hattie to speak, threw her hands into the air and strutted away.

Hattie turned to the young girl wearing the plum dress. "Is w-w-what the woman...said true?"

"No," the blonde girl sneered. "Josie had this selected for me." She pulled back the strap and showed a note pinned with her name, *Prudence*. "I'm insulted that you'd even question me."

Hattie looked at the note, but suspected that the young girl, with her lips pursed as if squelching a smirk, was deceitful.

Mrs. Bailey walked over with the older woman behind her. Hattie tried to explain but only stutters spilled out. The young girl stepped to Mrs. Bailey, showing her the pinned note.

"Hattie," Mrs. Bailey blurted. "This dress should have been pulled." She turned to the older woman again.

"I'm terribly sorry. We'll give you a five percent markdown on any gown in the store."

As the woman and Mrs. Bailey walked away, Josie rushed over to her friend. "Prudence, how lovely you look in that color. Sorry, I forgot to mark it for you."

"No problem. I did it myself. I saw it hanging in the fitting room and pinned my name to the tag."

Hattie rolled her eyes and headed back to her counter. "I c-c-can't do this much longer," she told her young nieces. "So much needless commotion: women f-f-fighting like alley cats and Josie's...dishonest friends."

"That's Prudence," Eva said. "*Prudish priggish Prudence puckered a pickled purple prune.*"

Hattie laughed, chuckling as she repeated the rhyme. "You g-g-girls always lift my spirits. And you, Eva, with your...tongue twisters."

Mrs. Bailey marched over. "Hattie," she said, handing her three gowns. "These must be steamed at the laundry. Right away."

AFTER DROPPING OFF the gowns, Hattie spotted unusual signage on the display windows of the next-door store and walked over to it:

MAGIC HEALER

She spun around when she heard a man's voice behind her. "May I help you?" he said.

The towering bulky man had tufty gray eyebrows, mutton-chop sideburns, and clean-shaven face.

"N-n-no. Just r-r-reading."

He gazed down at her. "I can help with that."

"W-w-what?"

"The stuttering. I'm an expert with hypnosis and mesmerizing."

She studied his face, wondering if he was a hoax. He studied her as well and then he bowed. "I'm Professor W. B. Wilson, Magic Healer. Do you want to give it a try?"

Hattie gulped. "N-n-now?"

"Why not. I'm in between appointments," he said, stepping around her and unlocking his door.

"N-n-no, thank you. It's b-b-been a very unnerving d-d-day."

He turned. "If you're worried about the cost, I normally charge fifty cents for an hour session, but could do a half-hour for twenty-five cents."

"N-n-no," said Hattie, backing away. "I didn't bring any m-m-money."

"Tell you what," he said, "let me work on you for fifteen minutes. Won't charge you a penny."

Hattie stopped mid-step and gave him a suspicious stare. "How's that g-g-going to help?"

"Should calm your stuttering the rest of today, maybe into tomorrow. And it will give you a feel for how hypnosis works. What do you have to lose?"

She pondered, biting her lip.

"Not going to force you. Have a good day."

"Wait," Hattie said, stopping him from closing his door. "You r-r-really think you c-c-can help me?"

"I do. All it takes is courage for you to try."

Hattie swallowed the lump in her throat and slowly approached.

"This way," he said, leading her into his back room perfumed with sweet exotic smells, which calmed her immediately. He pointed to a comfortable chair. "Breathe in the incense and try to relax." Then, in a low, soothing voice, he instructed her to listen to his commands. "I'll start off about five feet in front of you and move forward until I'm close enough to touch your head. Listen to my words and keep your eyes fixed on my two fingers until you're in a vacant stare."

Hattie nodded, watching him intently.

"You're walking backwards, step by step into the night. Fog appears. You bump into an old growth tree. Do you see the monkey hanging from the tree limb?"

Hattie giggled. "N-n-no."

"Focus," he told her. "Do you see the monkey?" he said, inching toward her and asking the same question.

Hattie concentrated. Suddenly, her eyes blurred and a long skinny tail appeared. "Y-y-yes."

"Now close your eyes tightly and listen closely." His soothing voice repeated, "You're getting sleepy." With his replicating words, she felt herself falling into a trance. Placing his hand to her head, he gave her instructions. "Holding your forefinger high into the air when you talk, your stuttering will stop. On the count of three...*one, two, three*...open your eyes and tell me your name."

Squinting, Hattie sat completely still and half-asleep.

"Your name," he repeated.

"H-H-Hattie."

He placed his hand on her head again. "Try again, but hold your right forefinger in the air."

Holding her finger up, she uttered. "Hattie." She paused, shook her head as if she hadn't heard it right, and repeated it again. "Hattie." She gasped and stared at the professor. "How'd you do that?"

"Power of will, but won't last. Takes time to build it up. If you feel a stutter coming on, hold up your forefinger before you talk."

"O-o-okay."

"Up," he said, pointing to her hand. "Hold it up."

ON HER WAY BACK with the steamed dresses, Hattie pondered about willpower and suggestion. *Wouldn't that be something if this worked?*

Entering the store, Hattie faced Mrs. Bailey's scowl. "Where have you been? Now those have to be delivered."

"I-I," Hattie stopped and lifted her finger into the air. "I'm sorry. I'll take them in the morning."

Mrs. Bailey looked at her strangely. "What's wrong with your hand?"

Hattie jerked her arm down to her side. "N-n-n." She stopped talking and slowly raised her finger into the air again. "Nothing."

"Stop that. Looks like hocus pocus. You're liable to make people think you're a witch. Your stuttering is bad enough. Don't need you adding more quirks."

CHAPTER FOURTEEN

THE FOLLOWING afternoon, Hattie's stuttering returned and the store's skeletal remains looked like the aftermath of a Thanksgiving turkey. The final orders to the vendors had been wired and the next shipment, which had been placed weeks ago, was expected any day. In the meantime, Hattie did her best to fill all the bare spaces with shoes, parasols, and wraps.

Time to take a breather, she decided heading to the back. When she stepped through the curtain into the stockroom, she saw that the holding rack was as barren as the store.

The day of the rush, some customers had their dresses placed on holding racks until they could return with proper payment. Hattie had stored her nieces' dresses there too with an attached *HOLD* notice listing each of their names. "Where are they?" she muttered under her breath, looking everywhere she could. She hurried back into the store and over to Mrs. Bailey at a clothing rack. "D-d-do you know what happened to my nieces' dresses...on the h-h-holding rack?"

"Got sold," Mrs. Bailey said.

"B-b-but, those were s-s-special ordered for the girls. I had them marked. I told Josie they were back there."

Hattie had helped her nieces select their dresses from the catalog. They were so excited when they finally arrived.

"Josie's the one who Okayed the sale," Mrs. Bailey said and added, "Mr. Veysey would've agreed."

"I see," said Hattie, doubting that her brother would have done such a thing, and she knew that Josie would have been outraged if it had been one of her dresses sold. She turned and walked toward the stairs.

Mrs. Bailey called out, "Where are you going? You have racks to straighten."

"I already finished." She grabbed her handbag and coat and headed out the backdoor.

On one of her daily walks, she had spotted a thrift shop tucked away on a side street. She hoped that she might find something for the girls that she could redesign.

She saw the store ahead and hurried to it. Once inside, its musty stench stuffed up her nose and she proceeded to the dress racks holding her hankie in case of a sneeze. She sorted through the clothes, but nothing stood out. Most were flowered dresses or plain frocks worn by older women.

A middle-aged clerk approached. "Can I help you find something?"

"Nice fabric frocks to make into p-p-party dresses."

"You're that good of a sewer?"

Hattie nodded.

Back home, her mother had taught Hattie to sew. Hattie even redesigned a wedding dress for a friend.

"Sorry," the clerk said. "Most of what we have is on these racks." She paused. "I do have two traveling trunks filled with old Vaudeville costumes. Can't guarantee the condition, but you're welcome to look."

"Y-y-yes," said Hattie, quickly following the woman into a back room of boxes, cases, and clothes piled in every available space.

"Over here," she said, leading to two large wardrobe trunks. "These have been here for years. Arrived shortly after I opened this store."

"You own this store?" asked Hattie.

"Yes," the woman answered as she and Hattie pushed the larger trunk out to the middle of the floor. The second smaller one was easier to maneuver and only required a couple pushes and pulls. "Take your time," the owner told her. "I'll check back shortly."

Ransacking through the small trunk, Hattie found sequined tops, hats, laced bodices, feathers and furs. She wasn't sure what she could do with them, but they were fascinating to see. It was the larger trunk that held the treasures: gowns of satins, taffetas, and silks, plus others.

"These must be f-f-from the eighteen-sixties. The fabric is superb," Hattie mumbled half-aloud, reaching for a lavender gown. *This color will be perfect for Mabs.* She spotted a purplish-red satin and gently pulled it out too.

"Find anything?" the storeowner asked, coming toward her. "What a beautiful color."

"It's called f-f-fuchsia," Hattie said. "How much for the two gowns?" She only had ten dollars to spare.

"Take whatever you can carry for five dollars. I only want the trunks. You're the first to have shown any interest." She touched the fuchsia gown. "Lovely."

"Yes, it will make a b-b-beautiful gown," Hattie replied, thinking of redesigning it for her own use.

"How I'd love to attend the Governor's Ball," the storeowner remarked, "but I can't afford a fancy dress." She paused. "Would you consider making me a dress out of this fabric? I'd give you all the items for *free*."

Hattie's eyes widened. "Free?" The woman nodded. Hattie's excitement grew.

She studied the middle-aged owner, trying to determine what style would flatter her pear shape. The old-fashioned gown certainly had enough fabric to design something nice. "I'll s-s-sure try."

"It's all I can ask. My name's Nora."

"And I'm H-H-Hattie."

THE NEXT MORNING on her way to the thrift shop, Hattie ran into Mr. Connell on his daily walk.

"You can keep them at our store," he told Hattie, referring to the thrift-store collection. She had cleared a space in her trunk to hide some of the garments too.

"Wh-wh-what about your son-in-law?"

"He won't mind," he said. "I've got the perfect spot in the back." He escorted Hattie to the Economy Store and into a tiny room with a treadle sewing machine. "You can sew here too. Let me grab the wheelbarrow and I'll help you transport the items."

When they got back to the Economy Store, Mr. Connell strung a rope across the tiny room's entry for Hattie to hang up the garments. As they unloaded the wheelbarrow, Hattie smelled the freshness of the old gowns and was surprised how well Nora's remedies had removed the musty scent.

Hattie thumbed through the Veysey fashion catalog she had brought with her that morning and found a dress with a similar drape to the old fuchsia gown. By late afternoon, Hattie had added an empire waist and redesigned the bodice.

Mr. Connell poked his head into Hattie's work area. "I'm locking up. How much longer for you?"

"Maybe a c-c-couple more hours. Is that okay?"

Hattie had left Mabs a note stating that she was helping Mr. Connell with his cow hopple and asked her to fix supper.

"Sew as long as you want," Mr. Connell said. "I'll bring down a plate of food shortly." Mr. Connell lived in the small quarters above the store. It had a hotplate, a single bed, and small closet. "The privy's just down the hall if you need it," he said, pointing to a door.

"Thank you," said Hattie.

Several hours later, Mr. Connell walked into the room. "What are you sewing now?" noticing that Nora's fuchsia gown was hanging on the makeshift clothesline.

"Mabs' dress," she said, holding up the lavender one. "Would it b-b-be all right if I work a while longer?"

"Take your time," he told her, picking up her empty soup bowl. He had brought her potato soup earlier. "Let me know when you're done and I'll walk you home."

"Will do," said Hattie, except she had lost time and didn't stop sewing until her eyes grew heavy. She lifted the lantern and looked at the pendant watch pinned to her dress and gasped. "Oh, no," she muttered. "Midnight." *I hope he didn't wait up for me.*

She quickly wrapped her shawl around her shoulders and tiptoed down the short hallway to the stairs that led up to Mr. Connell's loft, but saw no light shining from under the door. Relieved that he had gone to bed, she headed back to her little room, spread material scraps on the floor to sleep on, and covered herself with her coat.

CHAPTER FIFTEEN

AFTER THE LONG night at the Economy Store, Hattie got home in time to get the girls off to school, then she fell asleep on the sofa. A noise startled her awake. She leaped up, rushed to the door, and yanked it open.

A loud clanging merged with "HELP! HELP!" echoed from the store below.

"I'm c-c-coming," Hattie hollered, following Mrs. Bailey's voice.

A teller-like cage with metal bars, tucked under the staircase away from public view, housed a safe that kept all the earnings. Mrs. Bailey was locked inside the cage and continued clanging a tin cup across the cell-like bars until she saw Hattie, then she screamed, "We've been robbed." Gripping onto the bars with the cup dangling from her finger, she pointed to the opened safe.

"R-r-robbed?" said Hattie, staring at Mrs. Bailey in disbelief. She slowly turned around and scanned the store.

"Get me out of here," Mrs. Bailey demanded. "They threw the keys under one of the racks."

Hattie grabbed the baseball bat that her brother kept next to the cage, got down on all fours, and surveyed each clothing rack, looking underneath for any movement. She spotted the keys, pulled them to her, and hurried back to Mrs. Bailey.

"H-h-had to make sure they were g-g-gone," she said, fumbling with the cage lock.

"What were you going to do if they were still here?" Hattie gulped. "R-r-run for help."

"And leave me in the cage?"

"I w-w-wouldn't have done that." But truthfully, Hattie wasn't sure how she would've reacted. The instant the cage door opened, Mrs. Bailey flew out and latched onto Hattie's arm. "Wait here," said Hattie. "I'll go for the Sheriff."

"Not without me," she said, clutching harder onto Hattie's arm. "I want *out* of this store now."

Mrs. Bailey explained all the facts to the Sheriff and was so drained that a deputy had to escort her home. The Sheriff came back to the store with Hattie, but concluded that there was little that could be done.

"Any ideas on wh-wh-who...did this?" asked Hattie.

"Could be transients," the Sheriff said. "They come during hiring sprees at the logging camps. Might've heard that Mr. Veysey was away. How much did they get?"

"Twenty-five d-d-dollars and ch-ch-change. Do you think they'll...come b-b-back?"

"Not likely, but we'll keep a close eye."

The front door bell jingled. Hattie jumped and watched two women walk into the store.

"Better let you get to work," the Sheriff said. "I'll send a deputy by later to check on you."

Hattie nodded, but was suddenly aware that she must have looked a fright. She was still wearing her frock from yesterday and hadn't even fixed her hair.

The taller blonde woman of the two called out. "I'm interested in the pale-green dress in the window."

"I-I-I'll get it for you," said Hattie. After she handed the woman the dress, both she and her friend disappeared into the fitting room. Hattie rushed to the mirror to fix her hair and tried to brush out the wrinkles from her frock. From the little sleep she had gotten at the Economy Store, she could do little about the dark circles under her eyes.

The tall woman walked up to the counter and handed Hattie the dress. "It's too tight." She scanned the store. "Pickings are slim."

"We're expecting a d-d-delivery any day. Most are p-p-pre-orders, but there are a few scheduled for the racks."

The woman wrote out her name, address, and dress size. "Once the order comes in, notify me right away," she said. "If you see anything close to my size, please hold it."

Hattie wanted to tell her that she couldn't promise, but with the day she was having, it was easier just to nod and smile.

FOUR DAYS following the robbery, Mrs. Bailey sent word of fainting spells and was not sure when she'd be back, which forced Hattie to run the store until Josie got out of school.

When the front door opened, Hattie grabbed the bat resting on a small table behind the counter. Sadly, this had become her new routine. Relief washed through her when she saw that it was Nora.

"I heard about the robbery," Nora said. "How are you?"

"I'm a b-b-bit unnerved," said Hattie, "but I'm glad to see you. I have your gown." Hattie was anxious for Nora to see the extras she had added, like the glass beads to the bodice.

"That's why I stopped by," she admitted.

Just as she handed Nora the fuchsia gown to try on, three more women walked into the store. One of them was the tall blonde woman who had left her information with Hattie the day of the robbery.

"It's beautiful," said Nora, holding the dress against her body.

"That looks my size," the woman remarked, staring at Nora's dress, and then casting a glance to Hattie. "I asked you to notify me."

"It's n-n-not for sale," Hattie said. "I made it."

Nora interrupted. "I'll try it on now."

When Nora walked out of the fitting room, Hattie's jaw dropped. She knew the dress was nice, but couldn't believe how it outlined Nora's attributes and concealed her pear shape. "You l-l-look so lovely," Hattie remarked.

The tall blonde woman stared at Nora, then to Hattie. "Do you have any more gowns like that?"

"No. One of a k-k-kind."

The woman turned to her friends. "I need a gown with an empire waist. Look how it compliments her figure. She turned back to Nora. "I'll pay you thirty dollars for it."

Nora's mouth flew open. She froze before speaking. "Hattie, would you be offended if I sold it?"

Hattie stared at her, not quite believing what she was hearing. "Wh-wh-what about the ball? You were looking f-f-forward to it." She wanted to add that was why she had spent extra time adding special touches.

"Thirty dollars is more than I make in a month," said Nora. "I hope you understand," and then she turned to the tall blonde again. "Yes, I'll sell it to you."

Nora quickly changed out of the dress, handed it to the woman, and walked back to Hattie. "Business is business," she said. "It always comes first."

Hattie shrugged, but truthfully felt betrayed. "I'm surprised she'd...p-p-pay that much for homemade."

"Money's no concern to Leona Marshall," Nora replied. "Her husband owns five saloons."

Mrs. Marshall flowed out of the fitting room wearing the fuchsia dress. It draped the same on her as it had on Nora, but because of her height, even better. She stood at the long oval mirror, turning side to side. "It looks nice on me, don't you think?" asking the two women who accompanied her.

"Yes," one friend said. "That color is beautiful against your complexion."

Mrs. Marshall pulled out thirty dollars from her handbag and handed it to Nora.

Sadness crossed Nora's face. She looked at Hattie and sighed. "Thank you for making the dress. I wish I could have worn it." She grabbed her coat and hurried toward the door.

Hattie walked over to Mrs. Marshall. "Do you need any...adjustments?"

"No, it's perfect." Mrs. Marshall beamed. "Any fabric left?"

"Yes."

"Could you make me a cape? I'll pay you fifteen dollars."

"I'm b-b-backlogged," she said, thinking of Mabs' dress and maybe one for herself.

Lowering her eyes, the woman nodded. "I do understand. It was pushy of me to ask."

There was something about this woman, not snobbish like the others who had money. Hattie paused and cleared her throat. "No p-p-promises...but I'll try."

"Really," the woman said, touching Hattie's arm. "That would be wonderful, but I won't pressure you."

"WHAT A COMPLIMENT that someone paid that much for your work," said Mr. Connell. "When are you coming by to sew?"

"N-n-not sure I can. I'm the only one w-w-working the store until Josie comes in after school."

"Can you sew here at your store?"

"No, our s-s-sewing machine...needs repair."

Shortly after Mr. Connell had left, Hattie heard loud clattering outside, hurried to the display window, and saw Ivar and Mr. Connell pushing the pedal sewing machine along the planked walkway. She raced to the door and opened it. "What's going on?" she asked.

"We're building you a sewing station," said Mr. Connell. He and Ivar pushed the machine inside and back toward the stairs.

Ivar's head, still bandaged, brought Hattie concern. She had learned from Josie that he was supposed to take it easy to avoid dizziness. His face grew somber. "I heard about the robbery. If you're not feeling safe, just give a holler."

"Thank you, but I'm f-f-fine," said Hattie, not admitting that her nerves were still on high alert. "It's poor Mrs. B-B-Bailey who was confronted."

Mr. Connell knew that robbery talk put Hattie at unease and quickly diverted the conversation. "Ivar's a handy carpenter. Bet you didn't know that, did you?"

"No," she said. Her heart raced as she looked at Ivar, but she tried to fight it off. "I don't th-th-think Josie would approve of me sewing here."

Ivar interjected. "Don't worry. I'll handle Josie."

Hattie slowly nodded. "It would m-m-make things easier to work here, but your h-h-head, you shouldn't be hammering."

"I'm mended," Ivar said. "It's Mother who's making all the fuss. I slipped out when she wasn't looking. In fact, I was on my way here when Mr. Connell nabbed me." Ivar removed his bandage and stuffed it into his pocket. "That should have been off weeks ago, but the way my mother hovers, it wasn't worth the effort to challenge her."

"I see," said Hattie. She was happy to see Ivar and to find him well, but wondered if Mrs. Ekola might be giving her another talk. *Hope he doesn't mention me.*

Hours later, the men had transformed the alcove into an efficient, organized work area. Ivar even repaired the wobbly leg on the long slab table. They had shoved the broken sewing machine off to the side and placed the Connell one in its location.

"I d-d-don't know how to r-r-repay you both for such a...kind gift."

"Havin' you as a part of our lives is thanks enough. Isn't that right, Ivar?" said Mr. Connell.

"Sure is," said Ivar.

"I'll check on you tomorrow," Mr. Connell told her. "Good to see you, Ivar. Maybe now that you're better, you can visit Hattie too," he added, heading out the door.

Ivar grabbed Hattie's hand. "Speaking of visits, where were you? I waited every day."

"It was d-d-decided that your visitors be...limited."

He paused and studied her face. "Sounds like my mother and Josie's doing." When Hattie didn't answer, he nodded. "Well, I must admit Josie has been very sweet and caring. It's actually quite an attractive side to her. She even has her hair down and wears more casual attire like you, but you'd still never catch her in a frock."

Hattie smiled at his teasing. She had noticed Josie's changes in appearance, but certainly not in her attitude.

"And, of course, my mother is thrilled with the prospect of Josie. She's been so worried about me since the accident that it's actually nice seeing her happy again. And for now, it's just easier going along with her wishes."

Hattie looked up at the clock. "Two-thirty. Josie...will be here."

"Why don't you head upstairs," Ivar said, "and don't worry. I'll convince her to let you sew here."

"Okay," she said, pulling her hand out of Ivar's. He quickly grabbed it back. Her stomach tightened, sparking feelings that she thought had disappeared. "We have unfinished business to discuss."

"What?"

"The faller at the camp. What happened with you two?"

"Nothing," she said. "Never s-s-saw him again."

"Good."

"SO, THIS IS YOUR new workstation?" Josie said.

Hattie sighed under her breath and spun around in her chair. "Yes. Doesn't it...look n-n-nice?"

Josie shrugged. "Ivar does good work. He *persuaded* me to let you sew here. I have no problem with you making dresses for yourself. Just don't try to sell any in our store, like you did with those hankies. We have standards to maintain."

Hattie nodded.

Josie's gaze landed on one of the outdated fashions hanging on the rack. "What are those garments?" she said, coming closer. "Costumes?"

"Extras," answered Hattie.

Josie eyed the lavender gown in Hattie's lap and arched her brow. "That looks like a gown."

"Yes," said Hattie, holding it up.

"It'd better be for you and not Mabs."

"It's no d-d-different than you wearing one of Mrs. Cushman's altered d-d-dresses," Hattie quipped, biting her tongue soon as her words spilled out.

Josie gave her a suspicious stare and then an evil grin crossed her face. "Did Ivar tell you that he's taking me to the ball? He asked me tonight after a goodnight kiss. And what a kiss it was," she added. Josie was tickled to see that her news had upset Hattie. "I'm off to bed now," Josie added. "I've got plenty to fill my dreams tonight," smiling as she pranced toward the stairs.

Hattie leaned back in her chair, trying to erase the image of Josie in Ivar's arms, but she couldn't. Anger spurred inside of her and she wasn't sure if it was toward Josie or Ivar, or maybe even herself. *Why can't I break his hold on me?*

By late morning the next day, Hattie headed to her sewing station. Normally, she would have tidied up before going to bed, but she had worked late on Mabs' gown. As she gathered the cut-up material and spools of thread, she noticed an empty space on the clothing rack. She lowered her eyes to the floor to see if a garment had fallen, then back up to the bare spot again. What could be missing? She wondered, sliding the clothes back and forth. "Oh, no," she muttered. "Please not that." She frantically looked on the shelves, under the table, on the rack again, and then she raced to the stockroom, just in case she had misplaced it there. A dreaded realization hit the pit of her stomach: Josie left early this morning and the purple and gold clown costume, patterned with diamonds, circles, fringed tassels, and a double-layered ruffled neck, had vanished.

She knew the culprit had to be Josie.

But why would she take it?

CHAPTER SIXTEEN

SHE TRIED TO PUT the missing costume out of her thoughts, chalking it down as maybe a joke, but by the third day her anxiousness grew. On her way to the window display, she stopped short when Mrs. Cushman, Mrs. Wiggins, and Josie walked through the door.

Mrs. Cushman glanced at Mrs. Wiggins, who gave her a quick nod, and then Mrs. Cushman cleared her throat. "Hattie, we have an issue to discuss with you."

"All right," said Hattie, her pulse racing.

"This is a high-end store and we who patronize it cannot allow lower standards by you making outfits from costumes." She handed Hattie an envelope. "Here's a telegram from your brother explaining it all."

Hattie stuffed the telegram into her sleeve, turned, and caught Josie's glance. Josie stood motionless, sneering like a spiteful child who had conjured up a story.

"One more thing," Mrs. Cushman called out.

Hattie stopped and looked over her shoulder.

"Until Mrs. Bailey returns to work, Mrs. Wiggins and I will assist Josie with all items concerning the Governor's event. You can continue all other duties."

"Fine," said Hattie. She hurried to the stockroom, grabbed her coat, and shot out the backdoor.

Walking from block to block, she mulled over what had just happened, and when her mind traveled back to the present, she was surprised to find herself in Finn

Town. Up ahead she spotted a bench, headed to it, and sat down. She reached into her dress sleeve and tugged out the crumpled telegram addressed to Mrs. Cushman.

> **WESTERN UNION TELEGRAM**
>
> Received At: Transmitted From: Chehalis, WA
> Hoquiam, WA
> 11:00 a.m.   10/11/1903
>
> Madeline -
> No idea Hattie was making items.
> Will handle immediately.
> Appreciate assistance with large event.
> Thank you for update.
>
> Leon

Hattie rubbed her brow. *What must my brother think of me? Perhaps I should send a telegram to explain? But would it make any difference?*

When a woman's voice called out, Hattie darted her eyes upward. "Daphanie, you're back."

"I've been back for two days. Do you mind if I sit for a spell?"

Hattie hesitated. She was still reeling from what had just happened, but felt comforted seeing her friend. "Yes, please."

Hattie told her about Bert and the logging camp, but unknowingly, whenever she mentioned Nick or Ivar's name, her voice softened. Daphanie chuckled under her breath. "Nick sounds interesting, but not the type to hitch a buggy to."

Hattie agreed.

"Now Ivar's another issue. He's lucky you were there. It appears you two are very *special* friends."

Hattie blushed and quickly looked away.

"So," said Daphanie. "I heard that you've been making dresses."

"How d-d-do you know about...that?"

"I ran into Leona Marshall this morning. She's a good friend and went on and on about the beautiful dress that you made for her."

"Yes, but I made that d-d-dress for Nora," said Hattie, "but once Mrs. Marshall saw Nora wearing it, she w-w-wanted it for herself. She paid Nora more...than it was worth."

"Nonetheless, I bet you'll get others interested in wanting one of your dresses."

"No," said Hattie. "I can't." She paused and then sighed. "That's h-h-how I ended up here...today."

"Your dresses?"

"That gown was remade from an old...Vaudeville d-d-dress. Nora had two t-t-trunks with costumes."

"I'm guessing that the clown outfit was part of this Vaudeville find?" said Daphanie.

"You know about that?"

"The news surfaced yesterday."

"No wonder Mrs. Cushman wrote my brother." Hattie sighed. "I've t-t-tarnished the store."

"If anyone's to blame, it's Josie for showing that outfit to those uppity women. I wouldn't worry. Those biddies will be onto something else next week."

HEADING BACK to the store, Hattie detoured to the alley. She was praying that the stockroom door was still unlocked and was relieved to find that it was. She had finished Mrs. Marshall's cape last night and wanted to get it out of the store.

She quietly slipped through the door, dashed over to the long curtain separating the stockroom from the sales floor, and peaked out. She saw Josie at the front counter. Hattie needed to get to the workstation and back to the stockroom unseen.

When Josie turned her head, Hattie crouched down, crept over to a clothing rack, and darted into her work area. She was surprised to find that most of the Vaudeville items had been heaped into boxes. Grabbing the cape, she draped it over her arm and retraced her steps to the stockroom. She left Mabs a note in their agreed spot and headed out the door.

At the crest of the hill, Hattie spotted the Marshalls' red-brick house. It was exactly how Daphanie had described: magnificent views of Grays Harbor Bay and rose bushes of every pink hue. Hattie knocked at the door. It swung open and there stood Mrs. Marshall smiling.

At almost forty-years-old, she still possessed all of her beauty: ringlets slightly tousled and a curvaceous shape accentuated in a white lounging gown.

"Hello," said Mrs. Marshall, spying the covered cape draped over Hattie's arm. "Is that it?"

"Y-y-yes, but s-s-something has happened."

"Come in," she said. "Good timing, my husband just left. You can join me in a cup of tea."

Hattie quickly explained the town gossip concerning her sewing. Mrs. Marshall sighed and shook her head. "What fools. My great-aunt was a singer and traveled the circuit. Most of her gowns were made in Europe from the finest fabrics. Let me have a look at that cape."

Hattie removed the cover and handed her the cape.

"It's gorgeous," she gasped, placing the cape over her shoulders. "The fur is exquisite." Mrs. Marshall stroked it with her fingers. "You realize this is mink."

"That's wh-wh-what I thought, but wasn't sure."

"Those old-fashioned dresses and gowns that you acquired are treasures," remarked Mrs. Marshall. "With your skills, you turn them into jewels."

"That's not how the t-t-town women see it."

"Those busybodies don't know up from down. When they see me in your gown, their jaws will drop. My husband said I look twenty years younger in it."

"You d-d-did look lovely."

"As will you in one of your creations."

"I'm not s-s-sure I'll still be here."

The last letter from Hattie's brother Leon and his wife Mary stated that his back was almost healed. Hattie figured that once the quarantine lifted, which could be any time, they'd be home and she'd be heading back to Wisconsin.

"And if I am still here," said Hattie, "I don't need p-p-people whispering...bad things about the store."

"If they're whispering, I assure you it will be about how beautiful you look. You must sit with our group. I reserved two tables. We have plenty of extra seats."

Hattie shrugged.

Mrs. Marshall frowned. "I know how you feel. They look down on me, but my husband makes more money than most of their husbands combined." She clasped Hattie's hands. "I'll mark your name down."

Hattie stood. "I b-b-better be on my way."

"Thank you again," Mrs. Marshall said. "I'm so eager to wear your dress. It's nicer than any in the stores." She reached for her handbag and pulled out twenty-five dollars.

"We agreed...on fifteen."

"No. If I had to buy a mink cape like this from a store, it'd cost twice as much. I insist."

"HATTIE," MABS called out from the wagon. She yanked on Teaspoon's reins to stop. "Hurry."

"What's wrong?" Hattie asked, running up to her.

"Uncle Marion is at the store."

Marion, Hattie's second-oldest brother, managed the Elma Veysey Store. Hattie was to visit Marion with Charles after Charles returned from his trip.

Her excitement grew. *But why visit now?* And then she remembered the telegram: *Will handle immediately.*

Entering the store, Hattie saw Josie, Mrs. Bailey, and Mrs. Cushman talking to a slender man with thick brown hair speckled with gray. When she caught his gaze, he raced over to her. "Hattie Jane," he said, wrapping his arms around her.

Tears pooled in her eyes. "Marion, it's wonderful to s-s-see you." She hadn't realized how much she missed her brother until he was standing there.

He pulled her back. "What a beautiful young woman you've become. I can't believe it's been seven years." He put his arm around her shoulder. "How are Mother and Wallace? And the farm?" He shook his head. "What am I thinking? There will be plenty of time to talk on the train."

"T-t-train?"

"I'm taking you to the Aberdeen store," he said. "I prefer the train over the streetcar."

"Is Charles back?"

"No, but your help is needed there. Mrs. Bailey has agreed to come back to work, so there's no reason for you to stay here. Train leaves in an hour."

"An hour?"

"You'll return after Leon and Mary come home. No reason to pack too much."

Hattie gaped unbelievingly at her brother. She felt unsettled by his rush and hurt at how quickly she was being dismissed. "But the girls? I c-c-cook and clean."

"Mrs. Bailey's cousin will be helping with that."

"If this is about the...dresses, I c-c-can explain."

"Later," he said. "Get ready, please."

She knew not to buck her brother, especially since he had come all this way and it was obviously a decision made by Leon. She nodded and headed toward the stairs.

"You're leaving?" Mabs said. "But why?"

"I can't talk about it...now," said Hattie.

Eva interjected. "But we don't want you to go."

"You can't go," said Tillie, blocking the door.

"No, girls," said Hattie, her heart wrenching from the thought of leaving them. "It shouldn't be long. Probably no longer than a couple weeks."

Mabs saw how upset Hattie was and decided not to push. "Okay," she said. "We'll catch the streetcar and visit next week."

"I'd like that," said Hattie. She smiled at her younger nieces. "Go say h-h-hello to Uncle Marion. Tell him Mabs and I will be right down." She waited until they were out of earshot, then spoke. "I need you to c-c-cancel my treatment with Professor Wilson."

"The magic healer?" said Mabs.

"Yes. The appointment's tomorrow. I've seen him t-t-twice. He's helping me with my s-s-stuttering. I don't know why, but I was embarrassed to tell you."

"I understand," said Mabs. "Some people make fun of his therapy. Does it help?"

"Yes. His methods lessen my s-s-stuttering for a few hours. And it's wonderful to feel normal."

ON THE TRAIN, Marion turned to his sister with a serious expression on his face. "Leon and Mary appreciate all that you've done, but they also know about town gossip and didn't want you hurt by it."

Hattie blinked back tears.

"Don't fret, this will all blow over in a few weeks. You have to understand, Charles and Leon feature the Hoquiam store as high-end with only the finest fashions."

"Yes," said Hattie. She saw no need to explain her homemade hankies or the Vaudeville attire. Good intentions or not, she had overstepped. Her farm-girl skills and simple ways worked fine at the logging camp but not the case in an up-and-coming town. Marion's arrival and her quick departure made that point very clear.

The Country Store

Veysey's store was a country store,
With a barrel of dills against the door;
And it was the custom to gather in
Brown burlap bags that were not too thin.
And these old Veysey exchanged for any
Small trinkets in stock that sold for a penny.
His penny counter was bright with these:
Marbles; striped glassies; agates; crockies;
White peppermint hearts with "I Love You"
Printed upon them, too good to chew;
Licorice whips that would really crack;
Jelly beans in a barber-pole sack.

Veysey's store smelled of tanbark and
   leather
And was barnlike cold in winter weather;
And though I remember all about
The bobtailed cat he was never without,
Who napped at ease when he wasn't ratting
Where wheat had spilled on worn tea matting,
Old Veysey, behind two-by-four wicket cage,
Where he added, subtracted, added again
What you owed, or he owed, with his scratchy pen—
Old Veysey himself is a blur of age.
A face is irrelevant, or so it seems
When a child shops for spangle-coated dreams!

(Printed in the Aberdeen newspaper—early 1900s)

Figure 8
(Courtesy of Veysey Family Collection)

CHAPTER SEVENTEEN

LYING IN BED, Hattie stared up at the dark ceiling, rehashing all that happened. She had tried to fit in, but every attempt seemed to go bad. Even something as simple as making dresses. *What was I thinking?* She rolled over and fell asleep.

The next morning, she walked into the dining room and sat down at the table across from her brother. "Good morning," she said.

"Coffee?" he asked.

"Yes, please," said Hattie, scanning the small room. "These living quarters are n-n-nice. Not as big as Hoquiam's, but just as l-l-lavish."

"That's Nettie's doing," Marion said. He lowered his gaze to her face. "Hattie, I hope you know how much we all appreciate you being here."

She sighed. "I've made a m-m-mess of it all."

"Maybe a bit," he admitted, winking at her. "But Aberdeen can be a new start."

After breakfast, she followed Marion down the stairs into the store. It reminded her of the country stores back home. She peeked into the barrel against the window. It had pickles filled to the brim. A section of the front counter displayed glass-striped marbles, licorice whips, and jellybeans, to name a few. Canned goods and jarred food lined long shelves. Another section held mops, brooms, and buckets.

"My Elma store is similar," Marion said, following

his sister through the store, "and my living quarters are too, but my furnishings are not as posh."

Hattie nodded, half listening to her brother.

"Our country stores do very well financially," he added. "It was Hoquiam where Charles took a different twist, making it high-end to cater to all of the tourists heading to the beach resorts and the lumber barons' wives too. It worked out better than he figured. He and Leon are experts at picking out the right styles for that store."

"Charles has always had a g-g-good business mind," said Hattie. "And very...generous with his family."

"Yes," said Marion. "We are lucky to have him."

When Hattie heard keys unlocking the front door, she turned and watched a tall thin man with a long graying beard walk in.

"Albert Moak, meet my sister, Hattie," Marion said. "She'll be assisting you in the store."

The man gave her a quick nod and removed his coat.

Marion sensed Hattie's discomfort and quickly spoke. "Let her know what you need done," he told Mr. Moak. Before Marion could add more, the door squeaked open and a young woman with a small boy came in. The youngster darted for the penny counter.

Mr. Moak hurried over. "No sticky fingers on that candy unless you intend to buy it," he growled.

Hattie looked at Marion. "Not too friendly." She was used to Mrs. Bailey's cold shoulder toward her, but rarely with customers. In fact, Mrs. Bailey would go out of her way to be sociable. Mr. Moak seemed like an old schoolmaster. She wondered why Charles would want him running his store.

"He's an excellent manager," Marion said. "He used to have a store of his own and has been a big help to Charles."

"That's good," she remarked with hesitation.

"It is," Marion said. "Charles spreads himself too thin. Besides managing the Aberdeen and Montesano stores, he's on several Aberdeen town committees. Leon's arrival was a blessing too. He's as good, maybe even better than Charles when it comes to sales. I'm the lagging store of them all."

"I b-b-bet you're good too," said Hattie.

"I do fine, but not like them. Wallace and I were more suited for farming, but I like my sleepy-store life. After Charles returns, I'd like for you to come stay."

"That would be nice."

"How are you at bookkeeping?" he asked.

"Good. I've done the farm b-b-books for years."

"It'd be a big help if you could do the books here. Keeping the ledgers is the one thing that Mr. Moak doesn't do well. Let me get you started before I leave."

"Leave. When?"

"I have to catch the afternoon train," said Marion. "I need to check on the Montesano store. Nettie's father has been managing it in Charles' absence. If I'm lucky, I'll be back in Elma before nightfall." Elma was thirteen miles east of Montesano.

Hattie followed Marion to the teller cage at the back. It was identical to the one in the Hoquiam store: a small stand-alone room with oak on the bottom, brass bars on the top, and a side door with a lock. Inside was the desk and safe.

Mr. Moak meandered over. "What's going on?"

"Hattie's going to do the books," Marion said. "She's been handling them on the farm."

"Is that so?" Mr. Moak said in a grumpy tone.

She frowned and darted her eyes away again.

Marion blew out an exasperated sigh. "Look, you two. It's going to be awkward and the sooner you start talking to one another, it'll iron out, but I have to get back to my store."

After Marion left for the train, Mr. Moak had no need for Hattie's help. "Maybe tomorrow," he had said, "but I'm sure there must be some cooking or cleaning you can do upstairs."

"No," Hattie answered, annoyed by his old-fashioned views. "I think I'll get...some air." She wanted to enjoy the Indian summer day. Wisconsin had Indian summers too. Like this one, they were dry warm days at the end of fall.

Walking down Heron Street, Hattie noted that it went on for blocks with every type of business: grocery, jewelry, hotels, even an opera house, plus saloons and gaming parlors mixed amongst them. Almost every establishment had colorful advertising or striped awnings, but none stood out like the giant *V* in front of the Veysey Store. When she reached the Veysey block, sandwiched between F and G streets, she noticed the fire station off to the right and walked over to it.

In the front of the station was a cupola that housed a large cast-iron bell. Looking up at it, Hattie tried to read the inscription. She jumped when a man walked up behind her and said, "Quite a bell, isn't it?" She spun around and found herself face to face with a middle-aged man wearing a blue uniform. He continued talking, not even aware that he had startled her. "Once the bell starts clanging," he said, "it can wake the town clear up to the hills." He introduced himself as Fire Chief Koehler.

"H-H-Hattie...Veysey."

"Related to Charles?"

"Sister."

"That calls for a tour of my station." He walked her over to a barnlike structure full of carts and pointed to a horse-drawn one with a long tongue. "Old Tiger," he said, "best hand pumper around."

She learned that Old Tiger was purchased used from Oregon and had arrived to Aberdeen in 1889.

"On one of our fires," the fire chief continued, "the pulling crew didn't pay notice to the low tide and dropped the suction hose into the mud. They started pumping the handles, but nothing was coming out. One of the firemen, Old Rolli, saved the day. Wearing his rubber boots, he jumped into the river, carved out a trench for the tidewater to take hold, and within minutes, muck and water shot out of Old Tiger's nozzle. She's the most reliable equipment we have." He finished with a loud clap.

Hattie was thoroughly enjoying this man and his story. She could tell by his enthusiasm that he had many more to share. He pointed to buckets and helmets hanging on the wall, and then to another cart. "That's a steam pumper, but you need steam for it to work and that can take up to a half-hour or more. And sometimes you can't wait, so Old Tiger steps to the rescue again."

"Very...interesting," she said. She looked down at her brooch watch pinned to her dress and gasped when she saw that it was almost five o'clock. "I-I-I need to...go."

"Come back anytime. Give my hello to Charles."

She nodded and hurried back to the store. She saw Mr. Moak at the counter conversing with a customer and darted back to the cage. He had left receipts on the desk. She pulled out the ledger and began entering the figures. She hadn't noticed Mr. Moak until he rattled one of the bars. "How was your walk?"

"Good. I met the f-f-fire chief."

"He's a nice fella."

Hattie nodded and searched her brain for more to say, but an awkward lag happened instead.

"Everything okay with the books?" he asked.

"Y-y-yes," she said, without glancing up.

"Have to admit, you keeping up with them will be a big help." He turned around. "I'll be locking up in a few minutes. See you tomorrow."

THE ENSUING days became a blur. While Mr. Moak managed the store, Hattie worked on the books and exchanged small talk while he dusted the shelves.

During downtime, she yearned to see her nieces and to have her sewing would have helped too, but she was stuck to cleaning the living quarters, sweeping the store, and reading books from Charles' collection. She thought of Nick whenever she read a poem.

That morning while straightening shelves, she heard loud footsteps coming through the back door. She peered over her shoulder and gasped.

"Charles," she said, racing to him.

Charles, her oldest brother, was shorter and stockier than her other brothers but he was the most educated with a law degree. He had red-streaked hair, a bushy mustache, and a friendly, self-confident smile. Except for his city-man suit, he hadn't changed much since last year when he had visited the farm.

Stunned, Charles dropped his carrying bag. "Hattie? What are you doing here?"

"Marion brought me."

"Where is he?" Charles asked. Before she could answer, he wrapped his arms around her. "It's wonderful to see you."

"You too," she said. "Marion is b-b-back in Elma. Where is Nettie?" Nettie was Charles' new wife.

"In Montesano visiting her parents," he said. "Let me check in with Mr. Moak and have a look at the books, then we can catch up."

CHAPTER EIGHTEEN

ON HER WAY TO the stairs, Hattie glanced at the calendar on the back of the door: *Friday, October 16, 1903.* She shook her head in disbelief, now realizing that she had been in Washington for over two months. When she stepped into the store, she found Charles behind the counter. It was eight-thirty a.m., but it appeared to Hattie that her brother had been working for hours.

"Good morning," he said, looking up from the ledger. "You did a fine job on these books. I might just turn the accounting of all four stores over to you."

"Glad to help. What else c-c-can I do now?"

"Just got a delivery of jarred goods and a load of fresh vegetables. You could set those out. It's just you and me working the store today."

Hattie busied herself on the food and Charles filled the pickle barrel, then the grain and flour. He went from station to station, straightening and taking inventory.

"I smell s-s-smoke," said Hattie. When she stepped outside, she spotted flames billowing out of the top-floor windows of a giant building across the street. She stuck her head through the door opening. "Charles, fire!"

"What?" He dropped his clipboard on the counter and raced out to her.

Moments later, other merchants stood on the planked walkway watching in disbelief as thick black smoke funneled from a three-story building.

"Isn't that the Mack Building?" a shopkeeper asked.

"Yes," Charles answered. "Should've been torn down years ago. It's a fire trap."

The Mack Building, on the next block over, was one of the oldest in town and housed the Arctic Hotel, which provided cheap rooms. The building was next to the fire department and a rock's throw from the Veysey Store.

For the Veysey Store to be so close to the fire department and the Wishkah River, one might think they were safe from a fire, but Charles knew better. In addition to all of the attached wooden buildings, which was problematic enough, the wood-planked streets were built atop three feet of sawdust.

Hattie instantly thought of Fire Chief Koehler and wondered why the bell wasn't ringing. And where was Old Tiger, the hand pump that he had bragged about?

The Mack Building burst into flames. Timbers and walls crashed down with a roaring thunder. The fire leaped across the alley to the Walker Saloon, then to the Olympus, the variety house theater, which was catty-corner from the Veysey Store.

Hattie's heart pounded as she looked at her brother. Finally, the fire bell clanged and clanged. Then, the sixty-foot wooden hose tower that Fire Chief Koehler had proudly pointed out to her lit up like a giant firecracker. When the tower collapsed, crackling flames landed on the fire department headquarters. Within minutes, the entire block, bordered by Heron, Hume, F and G streets, was afire.

Charles hollered to the other storekeepers. "Start carrying your stock outside to the back alley. There's an empty parcel behind my building." He grabbed Hattie's arm and pulled her inside the store. "Take what you can. I'll get the ledgers."

Hattie gathered an armload of jarred food and raced out the back door. Other merchants were doing the same. When she ran back for more, she met Charles at the door with an armful. "One more load, then we go to the river."

It didn't take long before the once barren parcel looked like a dump heap. Charles, a natural leader, called out to the other shop owners. "One more pass-through into your store, then we head to the riverbank." But no sooner had he said it, when the fire jumped to Smits Drug Store on the corner. Charles grabbed Hattie's hand and the two double-stepped down the alley toward the Wishkah River. She looked over her shoulder and saw that the other shopkeepers were following close behind.

Crowds had already gathered near the bridge watching. Crying children grasped onto their mothers' long skirts, panicked women and men from a nearby boarding house stood helpless and confused, and shopkeepers dumped more goods into the middle of the street. Firefighters pumped Old Tiger and snaked the hose through the hordes and debris. Firemen, on the other end of the hose, tightened their grip on the nozzle as water spewed onto the flames.

When the large brick-faced building on the opposite corner burst into an inferno, Charles shook his head and looked at his sister. No words exchanged, but his eyes told it all as the large department store succumbed, leaving only two standing walls. He clasped Hattie's sleeve and pulled her to the center of the bridge, then handed her the satchel with ledgers. "If the fire moves closer, head over to the other side of the bridge, understand?"

"Wh-wh-where...?" Before she could finish her question, she helplessly watched as her brother elbowed closer to the fire and ran toward his store, disappearing inside. Her stomach gnawed. *What's he doing? Nothing's that important.* She saw him run out, carrying ten buckets, and sighed.

He hollered into the crowd. "Let's start a brigade."

Within seconds, a line of shoulder-to-shoulder men stood together. Two jumped into the river, dipping buckets and handing them up as the men passed them along. Charles, toward the front, doused their buildings with water. A back line with a handful of women, several scantily clad from the brothels, passed the empty buckets back to the river to refill. It reminded Hattie of when their old barn had caught fire and everyone joined in—men, women, and children too. She and Mother at the well cranked the bucket down to fill and cranked it up again, then poured the water into the helper's container.

Craning her neck back and forth to the fire and then to her brother, Hattie's nervousness grew. She spotted a man upstairs at his office window hammering an unrolled bolt of fabric onto his outside windowsill. The pit of her gut wrestled with worry. Charles and others standing below were screaming for the man to get out. "In a minute," is all he yelled back as he hurriedly loaded books onto the cloth to slide down to the street.

Charles and others gathered up his books. Hattie raced over and stuffed some into the satchel with the ledgers. When the man appeared at their side, relief and fatigue crossed his face. "These books are invaluable to my practice," he said.

Her brother squeezed the man's shoulder. "I know."

Hattie wondered if Charles was sorry that he hadn't thought to collect his law books too. Carrying the books, she walked with the man to the bridge and set the hardbacks at his feet. She covered her mouth with her hankie, trying not to breathe in more smoke now burning her throat and eyes.

The fire engulfed building after building, heading straight up their street. Hattie shook with fear. Suddenly, she saw chickens scurrying frantically between people's legs. She turned when she heard the high-pitch whinny of a horse. It was on a side street hooked to a wagon, kicking and elevating its head as its owner loaded his stock onto the buckboard. She looked toward the hazy street again at the giant "V"–the Veysey sign–standing alone like a ship's mast in fog and her brother next to it, throwing another pail of water at his building.

Hot embers rained from the sky. People opened umbrellas or held their hands over their heads, trying to fend off the fiery cinders. The man she had helped with the books handed her one of his larger volumes for protection. When a burning ember landed on a woman's shoulder, she screamed. A man brushed it off, but more floated down and onto his coat, which he quickly flung off but not before scorching his hand.

Charles hurriedly approached with a group of men. His clothes and hair were full of ash. He hugged Hattie tight when he reached her. "Our only hope now is the street's width," he said. "It's close to eighty feet wide and might work as a barrier."

Her lip quivered. She looked at her tired brother, fighting so hard for his business and for his town, but now all he could do was wait.

The fire had moved west, beyond G Street to Broadway with most of Heron Street flattened to rubble.

Figure 9
(Courtesy of Jones Photo Collection, Image 45448-1)
ABERDEEN FIRE (Oct 16, 1903)
Heron Street, between F & G streets

Note: Giant "V" VEYSEY sign on the RIGHT during the fire
(Old Tiger Fire Pump Cart on the LEFT)

The day after the fire, NINE businesses on Heron Street survived. One of those was the VEYSEY Store. Charles Veysey opened his doors, giving free groceries to anyone in need. [1]

Figure 10
(Courtesy of Jones Photo Collection, Image 4339-1)
ABERDEEN THE DAY AFTER (Oct 17, 1903)
Heron Street, between F & G streets

Note: Giant "V" VEYSEY sign still standing after the fire

---

[1] On the Harbor from Black Friday to Nirvana, John C. Hughes & Ryan, Teague Beckwith. Pg 12: Charles Veysey

CHAPTER NINETEEN

BY MORNING smoke hovered, making the burnt air thick and hard to breathe. Trudging along the ash-covered streets, Hattie held a hankie over her nose and mouth and Charles periodically kept his nose pressed against his sleeve. They had spent the night with friends, but were now heading back to the store. The Veysey Store was one of the nine that had not succumbed to the fire.

Along their route, they saw structure after structure heaped on the ground like charred firewood and sticky blackened grunge everywhere they looked. Tracks in the tar-colored soot reminded Hattie of footsteps after a fresh fall of snow, except these were black and polluted. She ached with sadness when she saw a woman in a tattered coat with three young boys, searching through the rubble.

Charles quickly approached them. "Did you lose something in the fire?"

"My mother's brooch," the woman answered. "We lived in the rooming house next to the Mack Building. We lost everything." She gushed into tears.

Hattie guessed that the slight woman was in her mid-thirties, and more than likely a widow who took in cleaning and sewing to survive.

"Come with me," Charles said, escorting the family toward the store. He hurriedly unlocked the door and motioned her and the children inside. "Take any food you want. It's free today." He pulled out a chair for her to sit and lit the potbellied stove. "Bit drafty in here, but will be warm before you know it."

"We're so grateful," she whispered, "and we are cold and hungry. I'm Mrs. Arnold and these are my boys, John, Elmer, and Frank."

SMOKE HAD SEEPED into the store and was giving Hattie a sore throat. "I'll get p-p-provisions," she told her brother. She headed to the stairs.

Inside the living quarters, the smoldering stench was worse upstairs than below. Holding a hankie to her face, Hattie gathered homemade bread, fresh-jarred jelly, and cheese and pickles. She hurried out the door.

Mrs. Arnold nibbled on the cheese as the boys devoured three jelly sandwiches. "Take some licorice whips too," Charles told the boys, before turning back to Mrs. Arnold. "You're welcome to stay as long as you like. I plan to be open until I run out of food."

"That's very kind of you," she said, rubbing her arms trying to warm. "You don't happen to know of any places that will take me with three children. I haven't much money."

"The W.C.T.U. set up a soup kitchen just around the corner," Charles said. "They're assisting with placement."

Hattie and Charles had stopped earlier at the W.C.T.U. (Woman's Christian Temperance Union) soup kitchen and hung a sign offering free food.

"People are opening their homes, setting up spare bedrooms or converting dining rooms," he added. "That might work for your family, but it'd probably be wise to go now to secure a spot. Use my name as a reference."

The woman nodded. "Appreciate your kindness. We'll go now. Come, children."

"And if they don't have accommodations, come back. We can make temporary arrangements in the store."

No sooner had Mrs. Arnold and the boys left when another family entered. They had seen Charles' sign: *Free groceries to anyone without food and shelter.* Charles handed them a box and pointed them to the shelves. "You're a good man," the father of four said.

When Eloise from the soup kitchen came into the store, Charles held a box as she loaded supplies. He threw in all the candy too, but her priority was carrots and potatoes for her beef stew. "It's sad to see," the older woman said, "so many displaced."

Charles called out to Hattie, who was at the back shelf stacking the last of their canned goods. "Watch the store. I'm carrying this food down to the soup kitchen for Eloise. I'll check on Mrs. Arnold, to see if she found a place."

"Is she the one with the three boys?" Eloise asked.

"Yes."

"Spinster Parker saw the three boys and snapped them up and their mother like they were relations. She lives alone in that six-bedroom house high on the hill. It's wonderful how people of all walks are helping. One family even rehabilitated an upstairs attic and another spruced up a back porch."

"What a day," Charles said, returning from the Mission. He wiped his forehead with the back of his hand. "Doesn't appear that we have much food left."

"Only a few c-c-cans of s-s-sardines and pickled herring," said Hattie.

"Might as well lock up," he said. "We'll spend tonight with the Martins again, but tomorrow you'll head back to Hoquiam."

Hattie hesitated. She wasn't sure how she felt about returning to Hoquiam. Yes, it would be wonderful to see her nieces and all her friends again, but not the gossips in town. "But what...about...you?" she asked.

She had noticed that her stuttering had worsened so she started stretching out her words, hoping to minimize it.

"I'll make up a bed in the store," said Charles.

"Sleep here...with all this... s-s-smoke?"

"It's already clearing out, besides, I'll be so busy with the cleanup of the town, I won't even notice it."

"Then I'll stay too," Hattie insisted.

"No. There's nothing for you to do here, but I could use your assistance with Leon's books. Marion left a note, said something looked out of sort."

"Really?" It shocked Hattie to hear that. "But Josie and the Baileys won't l-l-let me see the books." She had offered when she arrived.

"I'll send a messenger with instruction before you arrive. If the smoke gets too bad here, I'll stay in

Montesano with Nettie's parents and take the daily train back and forth. I do need to check in with my bride."

"Of course," said Hattie. "I'll head back to Hoquiam tomorrow."

CHAPTER TWENTY

ON HATTIE'S RETURN to Hoquiam, she had learned that Ivar had a relapse. She felt pulled to see him. The next morning, while strolling up the block and enjoying the warm Indian summer day, Hattie caught several women gawking and guessed it was due to town gossip of all her previous mishaps, but she wasn't bothered. Living through all of the devastation from the fire seemed to have lessened trivial concerns.

At the Ekola property, Hattie entered it through a wrought-iron gate and followed the brick-lined walkway to their large, white Victorian home. Her stomach wrenched with worry, now debating if it might have been better to have sent a note instead. She collected her courage, climbed up the steps to the wrap-around porch, and knocked on the door. Mrs. Ekola opened it. "Hattie?" she said in a strained tone. Her face showed annoyance.

"I heard that Ivar w-w-was ill."

Mrs. Ekola held up her hand. "He's much better. I'll let him know that you stopped." She quickly closed the door in Hattie's face.

Hattie sighed and shook her head. *Why did I think things might be different?* Starting down the steps, she heard the door creak open. Mrs. Ekola called out, "Hold on." Hattie turned to look. "A visit from you might be nice."

Hattie's gut bit with suspicion. First turned away, then abruptly invited in. She knew Mrs. Ekola rarely did things without motive, but decided to play along.

She followed Mrs. Ekola into the house, down a long hallway, and into the parlor. She paused when she saw Ivar sitting outside in the courtyard conversing and laughing with a strawberry-blonde young woman. Hattie immediately sensed her intrusion and searched for a reason to leave unnoticed. She looked at Mrs. Ekola. "Maybe this is a b-b-bad time."

"No," said Mrs. Ekola, nudging her forward to the window, and then announcing through the courtyard door, "Ivar, look who's here."

Ivar turned around, shock on his face. "Hattie?" He stood and walked to her.

Out of the corner of her eye, Hattie caught Mrs. Ekola, now on the sofa, watching the exchange. *Is she trying to make a point that I don't belong?*

"What a surprise," he said.

"I h-h-heard that you were ill."

"Nothing serious." He furrowed his brow. "Josie told me that you left, but she changed the subject so many times, that I quit asking. Where did you go?"

Hattie quickly explained how her brother had arrived to Hoquiam unexpectedly, needing her help in the Aberdeen store.

"You were there during the fire?" he asked.

"Yes," she said, giving him an overview. While they chatted, she could feel the young woman's eyes fixed on her. Her stuttering worsened. Before Hattie realized it, the young woman was at Ivar's side listening to their conversation.

"How awful to have witnessed all of that," Ivar said. "So glad that you're back."

Hattie smiled and nodded, but felt self-conscious at how closely she was being monitored by Ivar's guest and Mrs. Ekola.

The young woman interrupted. "I'm Kate. Ivar's college friend."

"I'm H-H-Hattie. Nice to m-m-meet you."

Kate was one grade above Ivar and had taken him under her wing, all under the guise of a study partner. Around campus, she was highly regarded as smart, ambitious, and calculating. Many admired her for that, and even Ivar found her refreshingly witty. She wasn't a natural beauty, but well-built and her tight dress enhanced every curve.

When Kate caught Ivar's eyes wandering back to Hattie, she wrapped her arm around Ivar's in a possessive manner and engaged him in a thought-provoking question: "Who is the superior inventor, Alexander Graham Bell or Thomas Edison?"

Ivar tossed his head back, laughing. "That could take hours to debate."

"Not even a clue of your preference?" Kate pestered, nuzzling up against him and forcing his attention back to her.

"No, but it will be a fun topic after dinner."

Hattie stood motionless as if she had disappeared and wishing more than ever that she hadn't come.

Kate then looked past Hattie to Ivar's mother on the sofa. "How gracious you have been to me, Mrs. Ekola. Here I arrive uninvited and you insist I stay."

Ivar had sent Kate a letter informing her of his accident and that he wouldn't be returning to college until next semester. Kate had arrived to his house the very next day.

"You're absolutely charming, Kate," Mrs. Ekola remarked, walking over and standing next to the young woman. "Ivar's such a scamp, never mentioning a friendship with such a lovely girl." She turned to Hattie. "Did Kate tell you that she's majoring in law, just like Ivar, and that her father is a judge?"

"H-h-how nice."

"What about you, Hattie?" asked Kate. "What do you do?"

"She can do about anything," Ivar said. "Should have seen her at the logging camp, she even nursed me back to health."

Kate raised an eyebrow. "Really?"

"Quite a special girl," he added.

Kate tightened her grip on Ivar's arm. "Am I a special girl?"

He looked at her confusingly. "I don't know. I suppose."

His mother interjected. "Of course you're special. He's never had a young lady so astute."

"I do pride myself on my intellect," Kate added. She turned to Hattie again. "Sounds as if you're a self-made girl. Do you plan to further your education?"

"Don't answer that," Ivar said. "It's the lawyer in her. She can't resist questioning."

"I sh-sh-should be going," said Hattie.

Ivar released Kate's arm from his and cupped his hand on Hattie's elbow, walking her to the door.

"I'm glad you're w-w-well," said Hattie.

Ivar reached for Hattie's hand and squeezed it. "I'll visit you in a few days."

"That would be nice," said Hattie, but deep down she wasn't so sure. To have seen him in an educated light with an educated girl made her feel inferior.

CHAPTER TWENTY-ONE

"ARE YOU ALL RIGHT?" said Mabs, rushing into the house behind Josie.

Josie plopped down onto the sofa and folded her arms across her chest. "Leave me alone."

"I've never heard Mrs. Cushman talk to you like that," Mabs said, standing in front of her sister.

Worried that this might turn into a spat, Hattie wiped her hands on her apron and walked out of the kitchen. She was thankful that her younger nieces were studying in their bedroom. "What's w-w-wrong?" Hattie asked.

Josie darted her eyes to Mabs and then she stared straight ahead. "None of your concern."

"Stop it, Josie," said Mabs. "Maybe she can help."

Josie sneered at her sister. "I don't want to talk about it." She jumped up, raced down to her parents' bedroom, and slammed the door.

Mabs shook her head and looked at Hattie. "I was in the stockroom. From what I heard, there's a problem with the hat order. Mrs. Cushman lashed out at Josie."

"But I thought Mrs. C-C-Cushman and Josie were h-h-handling it?"

Mabs shrugged.

"What about Mrs. B-B-Bailey? Why didn't she speak up?"

"Since the robbery, Mrs. Bailey's lost her backbone. Instead, she headed out the door. Mrs. Cushman was still so mad that she turned on Josie, saying that the whole store was incompetent and that she's pulling her order and might even sue."

"I b-b-better take a look at the...books. Do you know where the k-k-keys are to your father's desk?"

"No, but Josie does. I'll get them for you."

RIFLING THROUGH THE FOLDERS, Hattie located the hat order, laid it out on the desk, and scanned the first page. Every entry was evenly spaced for quantity, color, style, and cost. It all seemed in order, until she spotted the word *CREDIT* at the bottom next to the *eight-hundred-dollar* total. *Is this what Marion saw odd in the books?* She quickly opened the bank ledger and found an eight-hundred-dollar withdrawal. She stuffed the paperwork back into the folder and hurried to the stairs.

"Find anything?" Mabs asked Hattie.

"We need to talk to...Josie."

Mabs followed Hattie down the hall and knocked on the bedroom door. "Open up, Josie," Mabs said.

"Go away."

Hattie stepped closer. "Either you t-t-talk to us or I contact...Uncle Charles."

The door squeaked open with Josie's glum face peering out.

Hattie pushed the door wider, forcing Josie back. She walked in with Mabs and placed the hat-order folder on the bed. "This says c-c-credit and there's an eight-hundred-dollar withdrawal."

"Credit?" said Mabs, grabbing the paper. "You know how Father feels about credit."

"It was Mrs. Cushman," said Josie. "She took control. She said it wouldn't be a problem."

"Who withdrew the...money?" asked Hattie.

"Me," said Josie. "I brought the bank draft to the Baileys for signature."

"There's only two-hundred dollars in the account. That's much too low of a b-b-balance to run the store."

Josie explained that after the fire had happened, Governor McBride realigned his schedule, now giving full attention to Aberdeen. Mrs. McBride would visit Hoquiam and the Ladies Club reception on her own. This change resulted with the ball becoming secondary.

"The reception is a fundraiser for the fire victims," said Josie. "Those wearing our hats will pay extra to the fund. The governor's wife, Mrs. McBride, was so pleased that she sent a note to Mrs. Cushman thanking her for organizing such a worthwhile event."

"When is this all h-h-happening?" asked Hattie.

"Less than three weeks. The ball will be first, next Saturday. Mrs. McBride's reception is the week after that. With so much planning needed, we couldn't wait for payment on the hats."

"Unbelievable," said Mabs. "You harangued me for giving small credits, but eight-hundred-dollars, not an issue? Mrs. Cushman should've paid for it in advance. She's rich."

Josie wrung her hands and looked down at the floor. If it had been any of her other nieces, Hattie would have consoled her with a hug or encouraging word, but Josie's bite was too unpredictable.

"Let's see if we can get this...fixed," said Hattie.

Josie looked up, dabbing her wet cheeks with her hankie. "You really think we can?" she asked. "It'd be wonderful if you could."

"Worth a t-t-try."

"Are you going to tell Uncle Charles?"

"I'm h-h-hoping we won't have to. He's got so much going on after the fire."

As Josie exposed Mr. Bailey's involvement, Hattie's concern grew. Josie stated that *Mr. Bailey* had placed the order and wired the money, not Mrs. Bailey, she was still too fragile from the robbery.

"I thought Mr. B-B-Bailey was ill," said Hattie.

"He seemed better and eager to help. Last we heard the shipment was scheduled to arrive any day."

"Has he f-f-followed up?" asked Hattie.

Josie's lip quivered. "No, he left town."

"What?" Hattie and Mabs said in unison.

"I feel bad enough," said Josie. "I don't need the two of you making me feel worse." She lifted her hankie to her face and broke into a sob.

Mabs rolled her eyes at Hattie as the two waited for Josie to calm. Finally, Josie spoke.

"Mrs. Bailey had a breakdown when she saw the books," Josie said. "She asked me *not* to tell anyone until she had a chance to review it further."

"When was that?" asked Hattie.

"Three days ago. She's been trying to track Mr.

Bailey down. All his note said was that he's going to see family in California. She has no idea who that might be."

Hattie glanced at Mabs, then back to Josie. "We'll send a t-t-telegram to the vendor in the morning."

Walking out of the bedroom with Hattie, Mabs whispered, "Sounds fishy, doesn't it?"

"Yes, but it's best not to accuse...until we have all the facts." But Hattie's suspicions had already gone well beyond that.

THE NEXT morning, Hattie solicited the telegraph manager, Mr. Roberts, for assistance. She paid a small fee for research and waited until the final reply had arrived. He motioned her into his office.

"Appears only three-hundred dollars was sent to the vendor," Mr. Roberts told her. "The order left by steamer over a week and a half ago. It should have already arrived." He studied the paper closer. "That's odd. It shows that it shipped to Aberdeen."

"Wh-wh-what?" said Hattie. "Why there?"

"Don't know," he answered. "If it did arrive, I doubt if anything's left of it after the fire."

Hattie nodded, trying to remember if the blaze had reached the wharf, but she was equally concerned as to what had happened to the missing five-hundred dollars.

When Hattie returned to the store, Mrs. Bailey pounced. "What did you find out?"

"Only three-hundred dollars got s-s-sent," replied Hattie, "What happened to the remaining five-hundred? Did Mr. Bailey place an order with another v-v-vendor?"

Mrs. Bailey wrinkled her brow. "He must have."

"There's no p-p-paperwork showing that."

"Are you calling my Wilber a thief?"

"No, but five-hundred dollars is missing. Have you s-s-searched your house for an invoice?"

"Nothing's there," she snapped.

"Do you know why he w-w-would have had this small order shipped...to Aberdeen?"

Mrs. Bailey bore her eyes into Hattie's. "I'm sure there's an explanation, but I'm not going to stand here and have my husband accused of shenanigans. You can manage this store on your own. I quit."

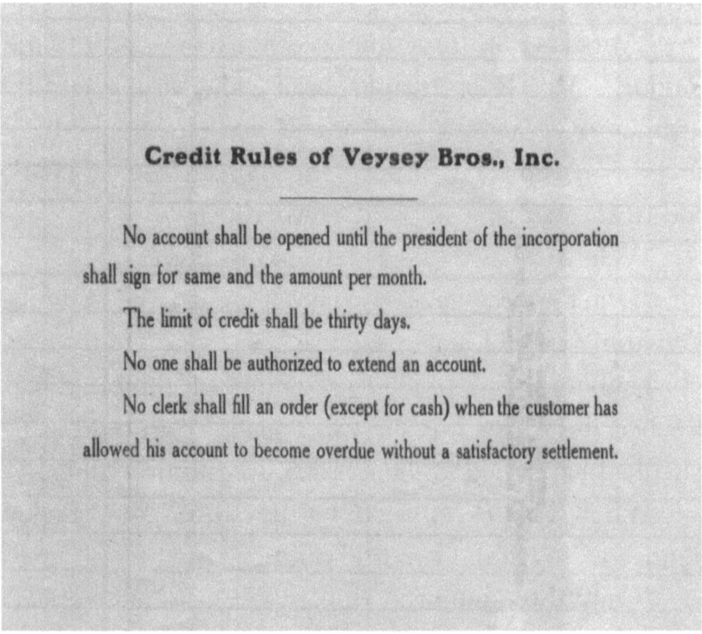

Credit Rules of Veysey Bros., Inc.

No account shall be opened until the president of the incorporation shall sign for same and the amount per month.

The limit of credit shall be thirty days.

No one shall be authorized to extend an account.

No clerk shall fill an order (except for cash) when the customer has allowed his account to become overdue without a satisfactory settlement.

Figure 11
(Courtesy of Veysey Family Collection)
(Early 1900's)

CHAPTER TWENTY-TWO

"SHENANIGANS? I think the word is crook," Daphanie said. "He had it shipped to Aberdeen to buy time so he could get out of town. That old bat knows it too. I wouldn't be surprised if she's packing up right now."

"I don't think sh-sh-she knew," said Hattie.

"You're probably right, but she won't want to be weaved into the snarl."

"It is a mess," said Hattie. "Will you c-c-come with me to the Aberdeen wharf to check on that shipment?"

"Sure," said Daphanie, "but we don't need to go to Aberdeen. I have connections here that might help."

When they reached the Hoquiam dock, Daphanie clutched Hattie's arm and the two meandered around boxes and crates.

"Olli," Daphanie called out.

"Hi, Daphanie," he said, wiping his dirty hands on his overalls. He glanced at Hattie. "Hey, it's you." He pulled up his pant leg. "I'm sure enjoying your socks."

Daphanie looked at Hattie quizzically then refocused on Olli. "We need a favor." After she explained, Olli nodded, but Daphanie didn't stop there. "We think Bailey pocketed the money."

"Daphanie," Hattie scolded. "That can't get out."

"I won't tell," said Olli, "but that Bailey is a shyster, always trying to get the men into a game of craps."

"Do you have any contacts in Aberdeen who can search the wharf?" asked Daphanie.

"My shift ends in a half hour. I'll catch the ferry and head over to Aberdeen and do it myself."

Daphanie winked at Olli. "We'll owe you big."

"You've lent a hand to me and Ma so many times, I've lost count. It's nice that I can do something for you. I should be back within three hours or so."

"I'm heading b-b-back to reopen the store," said Hattie. "I'll w-w-wait for you. I'm the only one working, so come through the front door."

Walking with Daphanie, Hattie learned that Olli's father had died in a logging accident shortly after the family had arrived from Finland. Olli and his older brother Jona had to work odd jobs after school to support the family.

"His brother got hired full time at the saw mill," said Daphanie. "He's married now with a place of his own and a baby on the way. He has an older married sister too, living in Oregon."

"How nice they made their way to a new start."

"Yes, but now all the weight falls on Olli. He was offered a scholarship from the Finnish Templars to attend the University of Washington, but had to turn it down."

"Sorry to hear that," said Hattie.

"Olli's resourceful. He'll land on his feet."

"Thank you for all your h-h-help today," Hattie told Daphanie. "I need to check on a m-m-message at the telegraph office... we'll part here."

She had stopped earlier to dispatch a message to Charles, but quickly discovered that the burnt telephone poles had cut off all communication to Aberdeen, so she sent the message to Marion in Elma instead.

Hattie walked into the telegraph office and immediately caught the clerk's eye. "Got your reply," he told her, pulling it out of a mail slot and handing it to her.

> **WESTERN UNION TELEGRAM**
>
> Received At: Transmitted From:
> Hoquiam, WA 10/19/1903   Elma, WA 1:00 p.m.
>
> Hattie-
> Charles is in Seattle. Not available. Inform Mr. Franklin, Bank Mgr, to remove Baileys from account. Get their keys. Keep me updated. Do what YOU think best. Grateful you're there.
>
> Marion

She stopped at the bank next, then headed to the store and found the front door unlocked. She slowly entered and saw Josie and Mrs. Bailey at the counter.

Josie came toward her. "How dare you treat Mrs. Bailey in such a manner. She's like family."

Hattie sighed. "Mrs. Bailey... quit."

"I was upset," Mrs. Bailey blurted.

Hattie squared her shoulders. "I informed my brother about the sh-sh-shipment." Her stomach was shaking like jelly, but she held strong, keeping her composure. "Your names are off the accounts...and he wants your keys."

"Josie gasped. "Who put you in charge?"

"It's all right, Josie," Mrs. Bailey said, digging through her handbag. "This will all straighten out when your father returns."

"Hopefully *she'll* be gone by then," said Josie.

Hattie ignored her niece and looked at Mrs. Bailey again. "Did Mr. B-B-Bailey have keys too?"

"No," she said, dropping her keys on the counter. She turned to Josie. "I'm so glad that you had left school early today, so we could talk."

"Me too," said Josie, hugging her.

Hattie held back her words. She questioned Josie's thinking, but quickly realized that Josie's spoiled nature had dwarfed her of any common sense.

Mrs. Bailey left. Josie erupted. "You're such a liar. You said you wouldn't contact Uncle Charles. I knew I couldn't trust you."

"I had no choice...there's m-m-missing money and more to the story."

"Mrs. Bailey explained all of that. Mr. Bailey placed another order. It should be arriving any day."

"Is there p-p-proof of that?"

"Her word is proof enough. You can handle the store on your own. I'm going to see Ivar."

Before Josie reached the door, Hattie called out to her. "When did you l-l-last visit Ivar...at the house?" Even though Josie's actions were intolerable at times,

Hattie didn't want her getting hurt and she knew that an unprepared Josie would be easy prey for Kate.

Josie arched her eyebrow. "Why?"

"Have you m-m-met Kate?"

"What are you talking about?"

"Ivar's c-c-college friend. I met her yesterday."

Concern crossed Josie's face. "What's she like?"

"W-w-worldly and smart."

"Is she pretty?"

"She knows how to b-b-bring out her best and goes after... what she wants."

"And what might that be?"

Hattie shrugged, but her message was clear: this girl was after Ivar.

The shock on Josie's face radiated more alarm, but more importantly, that she understood. "We'll see about that," she huffed. She pulled the door open and stomped out.

HOURS LATER, OLLI maneuvered a crate through the door. Hattie hurried to him. "You found it."

"It was piled with a group of others. It's in bad shape," he said, following her to the stockroom.

He pushed the crate against the wall, grabbed a nearby crowbar, and pried off the crate's top. Reaching inside the wooden box and through straw stuffing, he pulled out a crumpled wide-brim hat.

"Whoever packed this order did a lousy job," he said, digging through more packing until he found a hat that appeared unharmed.

"How about we s-s-set them all out...for a better look?" said Hattie, clearing off the stockroom table.

Olli handed her each hat and she examined them one by one. They counted twenty-five damaged beyond repair, fifteen not so bad, and twenty that seemed to be in perfect shape. Hattie looked at Mrs. Cushman's order and sighed. "There's s-s-supposed to be only thirteen yellow hats and they sent...twenty."

"At least they're in good condition. Can you fix the others?"

"I don't know," she said, looking at the not-so-bad blue ones. "But the c-c-count on all of these is off."

"A hat's a hat, isn't it?" he asked.

Hattie paused, wishing it was that simple.

"Can't you make some of the yellow ones, blue?"

She pondered his reasoning. "I-I-I could try, but if Josie ever f-f-found out..."

He rolled his eyes. "Is the Queen of Sheba giving you trouble?"

She knew he was referring to Josie and nodded, but it wasn't only Josie. Every time Hattie ventured out, thinking she was making things better, it turned out for the worse: the hankies, the dresses. *Maybe I should just accept the loss and leave it be.*

"How about I take these damaged hats over to Daphanie's?" Olli offered. "I'll fill her in and maybe the two of you can come up with a plan."

"Thank you, yes. I guess there's n-n-no harm in that. I'll keep several hats to s-s-see what I can do with them."

Hattie hurried upstairs and pulled Mabs aside. She

had told Mabs earlier that Olli might be bringing by a shipment and that she'd follow up with details later. "Where are your sisters?"

"In their bedroom," Mabs said. "This sounds serious. Should I be sitting down?"

"Maybe," said Hattie, leading her to the dining-room table. Hattie explained the missing five-hundred dollars, the partial order, Mrs. Bailey quitting, and Josie's reaction to it all.

"What are we going to do?" said Mabs.

"I could t-t-try to fix the hats." Her mother had taught her how to make cloth flowers. "But we can't tell Josie."

AT HER WORKSTATION, Hattie re-read Marion's telegram: *Do what YOU think is best.* She pondered. *The hats are new, they're just damaged. And we can't afford to lose any more money. I have to try.*

She opened the boxes filled with Vaudeville items, pulled out two blue satin gowns, and laid them out on her worktable. After cutting the dark-blue fabric into petal shapes, she held the petals above a candle to crinkle the edges and stitched a mix of them together. With light-blue satin and netting tacked to the crown and brim of the hat, she added the cloth flowers. It surprised her how much nicer the hat looked than the original.

Mabs walked in and set down a tray. Her eyes strayed to Hattie's lap. "Is that your redesign?" Hattie nodded. "It's stunning. I like how you left some yellow on it. Really adds flair."

"Let's hope they all t-t-turn out so nice and that Mrs. Cushman doesn't mind that they're...a different design."

"You're not going to tell her the truth, are you?"

Hattie shook her head. "I'm hoping we d-d-don't have to."

The next morning, Hattie placed a *Closed* sign in the store window, grabbed a large burlap sack she had filled with supplies and the two redesigned hats, and headed to Daphanie's. Daphanie saw Hattie coming and greeted her at the door.

"You've been busy," said Hattie, looking at the worktable in the middle of Daphanie's parlor.

Daphanie had organized the hats by color with the most crumpled ones in front. She had piles of lace and ribbons, plus scissors and various colors of thread.

"Olli explained it all," she said. "Thought I'd donate some of my mother's old sewing notions."

Hattie pulled out the two redesigned hats and handed them to Daphanie. "I f-f-fixed these last night, but we have so m-m-many more to do."

"Nice work," Daphanie said. "How about I get Olli's mother to help? She's a good sewer."

Hattie paused, calculating what she could afford from the twenty-five dollars that Mrs. Marshall had paid her for the cape. "Would fifty cents a h-h-hat be fair? I want to p-p-pay you too."

"Nothing for me," Daphanie insisted. "But that's more than fair for Mrs. Karvonen. I know they could use the money. Are you sure you can afford that much?"

"Yes."

"Okay, I'll get her over here now."

Waiting for Daphanie to return, Hattie stood at the table, pushed one section of the hats off to the side, and placed her supplies next to Daphanie's.

"Haloo," Mrs. Karvonen said, nodding to Hattie as she and Daphanie entered the room.

Her broken English reflected her Finnish heritage, as did her whitish-blonde hair, thin frame, and perceptive blue eyes, sizing up Hattie and the work before her.

"Nice to m-m-meet you, Mrs. Kar-vo-nen," said Hattie. "Olli is a wonderful young man."

"Olavi...yes, my special boy," remarked Mrs. Karvonen, sitting down in the chair beside Hattie. "Let's get to work."

Hattie provided step-by-step instruction for the petals. Mrs. Karvonen followed along, and by her third attempt, she had perfected a cloth flower as fine as Hattie's. Daphanie tried to make some, but it was quickly decided that she was better with tacking them onto the hats instead.

"You can c-c-cut the satin for the crowns," Hattie told Daphanie, "and tack those on too, plus cover the brims with lace."

Mrs. Karvonen lifted a caved-in hat. "Tsk, tsk. How to fix it?" she asked in her Finnish accent.

Hattie rummaged through her supplies, pulled out a piece of French embroidered lace, and formed it into a large bow. She placed it against the cave-in at the back of the hat. "What do you think?"

"Pretty," Mrs. Karvonen answered.

"But it'd be nicer if we edged it with a tiny strip of blue satin too," said Hattie.

"I can do," Mrs. Karvonen said, taking the hat and lace from Hattie.

Daphanie shook her head. "You sure have a knack, Hattie. All these hats look store-bought."

SATURDAY MORNING Mabs delivered the hats to Mrs. Cushman. Josie, still in a huff, refused to work with Hattie, so Hattie waited in the stockroom.

Mabs walked in with a widened grin.

"Well?" said Hattie, wringing her hands.

"Not only did she accept them," Mabs remarked. "She liked your redesigns better and she didn't mind that they were all different."

"I'm so relieved to h-h-hear that."

"She even hugged me," Mabs said, "and told me to have Josie stop by tonight." Mabs reached into her pocket and pulled out a bank draft. "Mrs. Cushman authorized a four-hundred-dollar transfer to our account. I'll take it to the bank."

"Yes, please," said Hattie. "That p-p-payment eases our loss to four-hundred instead of eight."

"Thank goodness you could fix those hats. Father will be so appreciative."

"Wish we could recover the r-r-rest of the money, but our only hope is if Mr. B-B-Bailey really placed that order with another vendor."

"But you don't believe that."

"No," sighed Hattie, "but Mrs. B-B-Bailey was

insistent that he did, so I'm g-g-going to give it two more days before I have to tell Mrs. Cushman."

Hattie walked to the bank with Mabs, then she headed off to Daphanie's on her own. She waved when she spotted her friend sitting in her front-porch swing.

"That smile tells it all," said Daphanie.

"Yes, but I couldn't have d-d-done it without you and Mrs. Karvonen."

"Glad to help. Ready to start on the fancy hats?"

"Not possible. There's no m-m-money or time to b-b-buy supplies or hats."

"Have you ever seen the painted ladies around town in their flamboyant hats?"

"Some have c-c-come into our store. They are colorful with all their b-b-boas and bright dresses." She didn't add that Mrs. Bailey always whispered about their questionable reputations the instant they walked out.

"I know several of them personally," Daphanie said. "I bet I could barter a deal for some of their old hats. You could restyle them."

Hattie shook her head. "No one will w-w-want to wear used hats and can you image if it ever l-l-leaked out where we got them?"

"You've made these into outstanding hats, and with your redesign, would fetch a pretty penny. Isn't it worth trying?"

"No, fixing the d-d-damaged hats was enough."

"Tell you what," said Daphanie, "while you drop off payment to Mrs. Karvonen, I'll search for one of my old fancy hats. Let's see what you can do with it."

CHAPTER TWENTY-THREE

HATTIE REDESIGNED Daphanie's fancy hat but only as an experiment, not with the intent of doing others. She had replaced the purple and red plumes with white ones, covered the crown and brim with pink satin and lace, and tacked a rose-colored bow to the back. That morning, Daphanie walked into the store wearing the hat. "I love it," she said.

"It did turn out n-n-nice," Hattie admitted. "It looks stunning on you." She didn't add that by toning down the colors, her friend wouldn't be mistaken for a painted lady.

"Then you're willing to remake the others?"

"No."

"Who's going to know, except for you and me? At least think about it."

HATTIE HEARD THE front-door bell ding and looked up at the clock. She had been so busy cleaning up her work area that it surprised her that two hours had passed since Daphanie's visit and that no other person had come into the store. She readied herself to greet the customer, stutter and all.

Hattie's stammering had become part of her daily store routine. Some of the patrons would linger nervously as she muddled through her words, others interrupted, and then there were those who just walked away and shopped on their own. Seeing that it was Daphanie and

Leona Marshall coming toward her, Hattie exhaled the breath she'd been holding.

"Your hat was the main topic at brunch," said Mrs. Marshall. "I must have one to match my cape."

"I told her who had owned them," said Daphanie.

"And I don't care. Will you make me one with the fuchsia fabric?"

"For you, Mrs. Marshall, yes," said Hattie.

"Wonderful," she said, "and Hattie, please call me Leona."

"Have you reconsidered on redesigning the other fancy hats?" Daphanie asked. "It'd recoup your loss from that louse pocketing your store's money."

"What's this?" Leona said.

Hattie explained that the bulk of Mrs. Cushman's hat order had not been placed and it appeared that Mr. Bailey had stolen the money.

Leona gasped, "Oh, my. Does Madeline know this?" Madeline was Mrs. Cushman's first name.

"No," said Hattie. "Maybe I should l-l-lock up and go see her now."

Leona sighed. "The Cushmans are in Seattle. Remaking the fancy hats might be your only option."

"If they were n-n-new hats," said Hattie, "or from someone else, but I can't chance tarnishing the store."

"Then don't sell the hats at this store," said Daphanie. "People can buy them direct from me."

Leona clapped her hands. "Perfect idea."

As much as Hattie wanted to recoup the stolen money, her gut was advising against it. "No," she said, "besides, there's n-n-no guarantee anyone will buy them."

"You've got my sale," said Leona, "and other buyers too, I bet. How much did that old geezer steal?"

"Five-hundred dollars," Hattie told her.

"Until we fixed the damaged hats," said Daphanie, "the store was at risk to lose another three-hundred dollars. Mrs. Cushman liked the redesigned ones better and was so relieved to get them."

Leona nodded. "I'm sure she was."

"But those were new hats," said Hattie.

"And you can remake used hats to look new as well," said Leona. "Daphanie's redesigned hat is proof of that. You'd be saving Madeline a lot of grief and your store from a large loss."

Hattie shook her head. "No, it's not w-w-worth the risk."

Leona frowned. "I understand, but there's more at stake than you realize. This upcoming event with the governor's wife involved has put Hoquiam on the map. A story appeared in the Seattle newspaper. Not having the extra revenue from these hats for the fire victims, which showed Hoquiam's generosity, could be a blemish against this town. Governor McBride is matching all donations received."

Hattie sighed. "And these f-f-fancy hats make that much of a difference?"

"They do," said Leona. "Ten fancy hats alone will bring in an extra five-hundred dollars. Remember, it's the rich women who'd be wearing them and donating an extra fifty dollars."

"And with Governor McBride doubling it, it's actually a thousand dollars," said Daphanie.

"Oh," said Hattie, her gut now gnawing on what she should do.

"In Wisconsin, didn't you do charity events?" asked Daphanie. "Like a quilt or baked goods to sell to help someone in need?"

"Yes."

"This is no different. And no one's going to know, except for us."

Hattie paused, debating every scenario that was popping into her head. "All right," she said, "but the only way I'll d-d-do it is if you donate ALL the money, less c-c-cost of the supplies, and no one knows I'm involved. And our store can't be m-m-mentioned at all."

"Agreed," both women said.

BY FRIDAY, HATTIE had redesigned twelve hats. When she heard the front-door bell, she jumped up from her chair, covered the hats with a sheet, and walked out to the sales floor. "Leona. S-s-so glad to see you. Come back here," Hattie told her.

At the workstation table, Hattie removed the sheet hiding the hats. Leona stepped forward and caught her breath as she scanned the hats. "What beauties," she remarked, reaching for a coffee-brown one. "What did this look like before you started?"

"Bright r-r-red with black and white plumes."

"Yes," she said, breaking into raucous laughter and clapping her hands. "Those ladies do cause quite a stir at the parades with all their bright colors, but what lovely hats they are now." Leona twirled the hat in her hand, turning it over to look inside. "Even added new lining. Did you know you had this talent?"

"I decorated some back home, but never as fancy as these." Hattie pointed to the chair. "Please sit," she said, handing her the fuchsia-colored hat.

"Hattie," she shrieked, spinning it to look at all sides. "It matches my cape perfectly."

Hattie had used the same fuchsia fabric used for her gown and cape. She added white ostrich feather plumes and a laced bow trimmed in mink.

"I must see it on," Leona said, jumping up and darting with it into the store.

"N-n-no," Hattie said, racing behind her. "You can't go out there."

"It's magnificent," Leona repeated, looking at her reflection in the full-length mirror. "Can you imagine Madeline Cushman's face if she ever discovered that these hats came from the painted ladies? She'd pucker like a prune."

"Is that so?" a shrill voice said behind them.

Hattie gasped and glanced in the mirror at Leona's shocked expression. The two slowly turned around to face Mrs. Wiggins standing before them.

Quickly removing the hat from her head, Leona handed it to Hattie, and then stepped forward. "Hello, Ann," she said, smiling through gritted teeth.

"Did I hear you right?" Mrs. Wiggins said. "Is that hat from one of those questionable women?"

"Heavens no," Leona quipped. "I was kidding."

"Didn't sound like it to me," the old gossip said. With eyebrows arched, she peered around Leona to Hattie with a what-have-you-been-up-to stare.

Hattie swallowed hard and glanced at Leona again, who now appeared lost for words.

"I'll see for myself," Mrs. Wiggins snapped, waddling toward the stockroom, but stopping mid-step when she spied hats sitting on Hattie's worktable. She headed to them, then she glared at Hattie. "Making homemade hats, just like you did with the dresses, huh?" She redirected her gaze. "How could you support this, Leona?"

"Hold your bucket," Leona said, marching toward her. "Madeline's hat order never came in, so Hattie stepped in to help. Look how beautiful the hats turned out?" She pointed to them.

"Baaa, I wouldn't be caught dead in one and neither will any of the ladies of this town. I'll make sure of that."

Hattie interjected. "I'm n-n-not selling them here. They're being donated and all money is going to the cause."

"They're still homemade," said Mrs. Wiggins, stomping toward the door.

"Oh, Hattie," Leona said, now on the verge of tears. "I'm so sorry. Why did I have to go out into the store wearing the hat?"

"It's all r-r-right," said Hattie, trying to mask her anger and suddenly wishing she'd never started any of it.

THE NEXT MORNING, Mrs. Cushman and Mrs. Wiggins strutted into the store. Mrs. Cushman's face reddened with anger as she talked. "How dare you pass off used hats as new," she said, setting down a paperboard box in front of Hattie. "I want my money refunded immediately."

With smugness pasted on her face, Mrs. Wiggins placed another box on the counter next to the one that Mrs. Cushman had put down. "These are the rest."

Hattie looked inside of both boxes and struggled for a response. "I'll r-r-refund the restyled ones," she told Mrs. Cushman. "They were d-d-damaged, but you owe for the others. Those were part of your original order."

"Fine," she huffed. "Separate those from the remakes." Hattie nodded and did as she asked. Mrs. Cushman turned to Mrs. Wiggins. "Are you available to go to Seattle now? We need to get a new hat order placed."

"Yes. I'll meet you at the train station within the hour."

CHAPTER TWENTY-FOUR

MABS RUSHED down the stairs into the store. "Hattie," she said, skidding to a stop. "An urgent telegram arrived for you." She handed it to Hattie.

It had been over a week since her hat encounter with Mrs. Cushman, but something in her gut told her this telegram was related. She gasped as she read it.

"What is it?" said Mabs.

"Your g-g-grandmother is arriving at f-f-four o'clock. Today!"

WAITING FOR THE TRAIN with her nieces, Hattie's stomach knotted. She was guessing that her brother Leon had sent a telegram prompting Mother to come. Even though her brother Charles reassured her not to worry about the ordeal with the hats, it was still Leon's store. Hattie was certain Mrs. Cushman had notified him.

When Mother stepped off the train and onto the platform, she craned her neck looking for a familiar face.

"Wait here," Hattie told the girls. She hurried to her mother and flung her arms around her.

"Hattie," Mother scolded. "Don't make such a fuss. You know I don't like public displays."

Stepping back, Hattie nodded and bumped into a ginger-haired man. "Excuse me," she said, glancing over her shoulder, but not giving the large man much notice, until he placed his hands on her waist and twisted her around to face him.

"Nothin' to excuse," he said as his eyes roved her up and down. "My, Hattie, what a beauty you've become."

Her eyes widened. "C-C-Cecil?"

Cecil, a boyhood friend of her brother Wallace was always a large boy with a round face, puffy eyes, and a lone patch of curls falling across his forehead. He hadn't changed much except he was broader.

"Your mother needed an escort, so I volunteered. Now give me a hug," he said, holding her tightly.

"Oh," said Hattie, squirming to get out of his grip.

Mother huffed. "You two can catch up later. Where are the girls?" Before Hattie could answer, Mother was heading toward Josie, who was making her way to her.

Josie curtsied. "Hello, Grandmother."

"Josephine, what a lovely young lady you've become," her grandmother said, extending Josie at arm's length to look at her. Mother turned to Hattie, who was now standing next to her. "She's more beautiful than her pictures and what proper etiquette and poise."

"Thank you, Grandmother," Josie responded sweetly. "I'd be happy to teach Hattie, any time."

Hattie felt heat rush to her cheeks when her mother answered, "That would be very nice, dear."

Mabs walked up. "I'm Mabel," she said, wobbling with a sideways curtsey.

Holding hands, Eva and Tillie shuffled forward next. "Evelyn," Eva mouthed, barely above a whisper.

When Tillie blurted out *Tillie*, her grandmother cast a disapproving glance at Hattie.

Hattie stepped to Tillie and clasped her hand. "The

children h-h-have nicknames. They're really quite...c-c-cute."

"Not around me," Mother said, looking down at Tillie. "You are to only use your proper name."

Tillie gulped. "Matilda."

Waiting for a porter to load her trunk into the Veysey wagon, Mother introduced Cecil to the girls. Hattie stood off to the side and looked at the station, recalling the day she had arrived.

"What's got your thoughts?" Cecil said, grasping Hattie's hand.

"Nothing." She quickly pulled her hand away, but not before catching Josie's watchful eyes.

"Seems you're fond of Hattie," Josie said to Cecil.

Hattie sighed. "We're old friends."

Mother interrupted. "Cecil needs a hotel."

"Normally, I'd suggest the Hoquiam Hotel," Josie said, pointing to the large structure across the street. "But it's booked for the ball this Saturday."

"A ball?" said Cecil. "Sounds like quite an event. Are you attending?"

"Yes," answered Josie. "We all are, except for my younger sisters."

He turned to Hattie. "You too?"

Before Hattie could answer, Josie spoke up. "Yes, but she doesn't have an escort."

Cecil put his arm around Hattie's shoulder. "Well she does now."

Hattie gasped and stared at Josie, who was smiling with her evil grin.

"She doesn't need one," said Mabs, staring down from the wagon seat. "I'm betting her dance card will be filled fast." Mabs glanced at Cecil. "The Harbor Manor. It's just up the street. Less than a ten-minute walk."

"Okay," he said, helping Mrs. Veysey up to the wagon. Then he turned to Hattie before she climbed aboard. "Perhaps you'll walk with me to the hotel and maybe share a bite to eat?"

"No," said Mother. "Hattie and I need to catch up. "Josephine, would you and the girls walk with Cecil?"

"We'd be happy to," said Josie. "It will be fun to learn more about Aunt Hattie."

Hattie held her tongue, but not her thoughts. She had always found Cecil arrogant and wished that he hadn't come.

His father owned the largest farm in Waupaca and Cecil thought he was better than others because his family was rich. Hattie never understood why Wallace considered him a friend. She fumed over the prospect of attending the ball with him. *How dare him. He's as pushy as ever.*

ON THE WAGON RIDE through town, Mother sat on the springboard seat between Hattie and Mabs, bobbing her head in one direction and then the opposite. Taking it all in like Hattie did when she arrived.

"Whoa," said Mabs, pulling on Teaspoon's reins. Mabs slid down off the wagon, tied her horse to the Veysey Store signpost, and then helped her grandmother down. Hattie managed on her own.

"I'll fetch Olli," said Mabs, "to help with the trunk." She walked away before her grandmother could respond.

Hattie's mother sighed. "No etiquette to wait until she's dismissed?"

Hattie ignored her mother. "This way," she said, unlocking the store and motioning her inside.

Her mother stood, shaking her head. "My sons have done well for themselves. But why are we at the store and not at their house?"

"They live above the store," said Hattie. Soon as they entered the living quarters, Mother's eyebrows arched. Hattie knew that judgments were being formed about Leon and Mary's lifestyle—especially, living above the store instead of a stand-alone house.

Mother sat down on the sofa. "Quite a fancy life," she said. "You certainly wouldn't know that Leon and Mary were raised on farms."

Hattie didn't want to admit that she had become accustomed to these finer things too. "Mother, would you like to f-f-freshen up or rest? We've prepared Leon and Mary's bedroom for you. I'll be s-s-sleeping on the sofa."

"No, I'll rest later," Mother said, sipping the water Hattie had poured. "Leon wired for me to come right away. He feels that you're overwhelmed. He mentioned some mix-up with hats too."

"I see," said Hattie, folding her hands in her lap.

"His concerns may have been right," Mother said. "Josie is wonderful, but the others need shaping. I'm especially concerned with Matilda. She's quite spirited. And Mabel needs some work too."

"N-n-no," Hattie said. "The girls are very sweet." She saw no point in bringing up the rubbish between her and Josie. "You'll c-c-come to love them."

Mother frowned. "What a silly thing to say. I already do love them."

"Of c-c-course," said Hattie.

Mother narrowed her eyes. "You look so different with your hair like that."

"Do you like it?" asked Hattie. Daphanie had styled Hattie's hair in a Gibson-girl up-do, puffed above the forehead and sides with a loose knot sitting atop. "I was told it c-c-complimented my face."

"Might be a good look for Josie, but you're a farm girl. It's best you keep it pulled back into a bun. I think that would please Cecil too."

"Cecil? Why should I care w-w-what he thinks?"

"I don't want to get into that discussion now."

"What discussion?"

Mother sighed heavily and reluctantly reached into her handbag. It's from Mr. Hickel." Cecil was Mr. Hickel's only son.

Hattie gave her mother a questioning look and slowly opened the letter. Reading, she gasped and stared up. "He talks about Cecil and me g-g-getting married."

"Mr. Hickel approached me last month. His greatest fear is no grandchildren before he dies. When I told him I was coming, he insisted Cecil escort me."

"Is Mr. Hickel sick?"

"He has some ailments, so one never knows. He's quite fond of you."

"I like him too," said Hattie, "but that d-d-doesn't mean I want to m-m-marry Cecil. He's not my type."

Mother's eyebrows shot up. "Since when do you have a type?"

Hattie squirmed. "He's at least t-t-ten years older and rather b-b-big." She didn't add that when he laughed, he snorted like a donkey.

"Mr. Hickel has one of the largest parcels in Waupaca and soon it'll all belong to Cecil," said Mother. "And most of Cecil's width is muscle from working the farm."

"Uh, huh," said Hattie. It was Cecil's father and the farmhands who worked the soil, not his lazy son.

Hattie slumped in her chair. She detested how her mother thought that she always knew best, planning for Hattie before she had a chance to say yes or no. "Does Wallace know any of this?"

"Never mind what your brother thinks. This is about you." She reached for Hattie's hand. "Cecil will treat you like royalty. Not many men would want a woman who stutters. He agreed to come, but made no guarantees. He seemed pleased when he saw you."

"I'm not m-m-marrying him, Mother."

"I see now that sending you here was a mistake. Being around Josie, with so much promise, has given you false hope. But you're a sensible girl. You'll see that I'm right."

At supper, the girls sat straight in their chairs and only talked when addressed. Hattie was still angry and kept quiet. It surprised her how much impact Mother's presence had on her nieces until she looked down at her own drab dress, realizing that Mother had affected her as well.

"We'll start a Bible study tomorrow night," Mother remarked, glancing at Hattie. "Every night after supper."

Josie cast a sideways glance at her sisters, then took a deep breath and spoke. "Grandmother, most evenings I visit Mrs. Cushman or I stop to see Mrs. Ekola. I'm courting her son."

Mother gazed across the table at Hattie. "Seems there are several items you didn't mention."

"Uh-uh-uh."

"Enough with the stuttering," she told her daughter. She turned back to Josie. "I'm getting a clearer picture of this situation and see that Hattie hasn't had full command. From now on, you'll come directly home."

"But my parents gave Mrs. Cushman permission to instruct me. I'm learning French."

"French? That's nonsense."

"Mrs. Cushman is a very prominent figure," Josie remarked haughtily. "She's married to a lumber baron."

Her grandmother narrowed her eyes. "Don't use that tone with me. Until I meet these people, there will be no more after-school visits."

CHAPTER TWENTY-FIVE

ON HIS THIRTY-FIRST BIRTHDAY, Cecil had decided that it was time to take a wife, but he had never considered Hattie. When his father proposed the idea, he brushed it off. "No," he had said. "She was always a pest, tagging along, and I found her stuttering annoying."

"She's not a child anymore," his father had remarked. "She's grown up quite fine. I think a pretty wife outweighs how she talks."

"Nope," Cecil told his father. "I can't imagine it. My first choice is Margaret Jackson or Beth Walters."

"Neither one will produce attractive children, but you've got a chance with Hattie. At least escort Mrs. Veysey out west and see for yourself."

Cecil agreed to come, but had also resolved that it'd be either Margaret or Beth as his bride. But now that he'd seen Hattie, he was reconsidering.

IT HAD BEEN two days since his arrival to Hoquiam and he had arranged with Mrs. Veysey for Hattie to join him for lunch.

At the knock at the door, Mother turned to Hattie. "Now remember this is just a getting-to-know-you visit. He's not rushing you off to get wed."

"H-h-hope he knows that," said Hattie, recalling how persistent Cecil used to be to get his way. "I don't want to be alone with him. Why don't you c-c-come along?"

"No," Mother said, opening the door.

"Hello," said Cecil, smiling as his eyes measured Hattie up and down. After they descended the stairs, Cecil latched onto her arm. "I passed a nice eatery."

"Sounds f-f-fine," said Hattie, trying to wiggle loose from his grip, but he tightened his hand instead.

"You look very pretty. I'm flattered that you'd make such an effort for me."

"W-w-what? No."

She had considered wearing her drabbest dress and pulling her hair into a tight bun, her mother's suggestion. Then she rationalized if the farm-girl look is what Cecil preferred, she'd be the opposite.

Oh yes, I like this new Hattie, Cecil thought as he seated her at the table.

Hattie placed a napkin into her lap. She glanced up and caught Cecil's wandering gaze. She blushed.

"My, Hattie," he said in a drooling tone. "You sure have blossomed. If looks were all a man needed in a wife, you'd win hands down."

"Please s-s-stop, Cecil. You're m-m-making me uncomfortable."

"Still have that stutter. Too bad, otherwise, you'd be at the top of the pile."

"What do you m-m-mean by that?"

"To marry, of course," he said. "I don't need good conversation if you can cook."

"I have n-n-no interest in being your wife."

"Same feisty girl. Now that could be fun."

"She threw her napkin onto her plate and stood. "You can eat b-b-by yourself."

A pompous sneer crossed his face. He never anticipated that a flawed girl like Hattie would reject the most sought-after bachelor in their county. *How dare she?* He cleared his throat and settled into a congenial smile. "You know that our parents are trying to push us together. I just wanted to see where you stood. Sorry for the misunderstanding."

Hattie studied his face. He sounded sincere, but she also knew how Cecil could persuade, recalling the time he had stolen a peppermint stick. At the very moment he was sliding it into his pocket, he convinced the shopkeeper that he had miscounted.

Cecil stood up. "I am sorry. Please sit."

"All right," she said reluctantly.

"Truthfully, I never considered you as a wife. I've been courting Beth Walters and Margaret Jackson."

Beth and Margaret, closer in age to Cecil, were both thrilled with the prospect of being his wife. Margaret would bake one of her special pies. Beth, not as good of a cook, enticed him behind the barn with romantic kisses.

"So you're g-g-going to pick one of them?" Hattie asked, trying to temper her excitement.

He slowly nodded. "But you know, Hattie. You could do a whole lot worse than me."

"I'm s-s-sorry if I offended you. I do c-c-consider you a friend. I don't want to...marry...anyone."

He leaned back in his chair, pretending to agree, but as he stared at her, he stewed even more. *She should be honored that I'd even consider her with her stutter. But*

I do like what I see and if I want you, Hattie, it's going to happen.

"Are you enjoying your visit here?" he asked.

She shrugged, debating on how to answer.

"Don't be shy," he said.

"Haven't g-g-given it much thought." But the truth was she had given it long and serious attention, and for a spell, had contemplated staying. At least that's how she felt before the recent hat incident. And a lot of her not wanting to leave had to do with Ivar.

CECIL MADE LUNCH plans with Mrs. Veysey the next day.

"I thought it might be best for us to talk privately," he said, helping her to her seat at the table. They were dining at an upscale eatery connected to his hotel.

"I'm guessing this has to do with Hattie," said Mrs. Veysey.

"Oh, yes," he said, nodding. "She's quite a girl."

"You want to expand on that?"

"I only came because my father kept pestering. I never had any interest in Hattie as a wife until I saw the grown-up package. But she's going to be hard to rope. I'm going to need your help."

"How's that?"

"May have to trick her," he said, "but really, I shouldn't have to, I'm quite a catch. Not sure if you know, but I already own sixty acres and will inherit another one-hundred-fifty when my father passes, but that will be years from now."

"I don't know, Cecil," Mrs. Veysey said. "She's not the same. The old Hattie would've listened to me, but working in a high-scale store has given her fancy ideas and she no longer resembles a farm girl."

"I've noticed and I like it just fine," he spouted.

"You do?"

"Yes. Her up-do hair and colorful clothes polish her new look. She can buy whatever makes her sparkle. All I insist on is at least two boys to carry on my name. In fact, I'd like a handful of little chickens, don't care if the rest are girls, and it'd be awful fun making them with her."

"Cecil," Mrs. Veysey said, now annoyed by his crude remark. She looked side to side to ensure that no one overheard.

The time Mrs. Veysey had spent with Cecil on the train had given her a broader view of him. Yes, he'd provide a good life and Hattie didn't have many husband prospects, in fact, not one. On those issues alone, Mrs. Veysey was willing to dismiss his uncouthness, which she had witnessed several times on their trip out. And Hattie couldn't ask for a better father-in-law than Mr. Hickel. That also pushed Cecil to the top. Mrs. Veysey hoped that once Cecil married, he'd grow up and some of his father's good traits and manners would rub off onto him.

"Here's my plan," said Cecil, telling Mrs. Veysey that he'd send Hattie and her to Chicago to rest and see the sights. He'd show up later and charm Hattie into falling for him.

"It's a bit far-fetched," Mrs. Veysey said. "And you make it all sound so easy. Love doesn't just happen."

He cleared his throat. "You'd be surprised what money can do. If she doesn't go for the trip, there's always another way to persuade. We could tell her that you're ill and it's forcing you to sell your farm to me."

"She won't believe that."

He blew out an exasperated breath and leaned back in his chair. "I don't understand your resistance. It was *you* and my father who wanted us married."

"Yes," said Mrs. Veysey, begrudgingly. Now wishing she hadn't entered into an agreement with Mr. Hickel.

"Most men wouldn't look twice at someone who stutters, even one as pretty as Hattie. But I'm willing to take her flawed, but she's too far from home to judge my merits, so we can't push. All I'm asking is that you get her back to Wisconsin."

CHAPTER TWENTY-SIX

THE NEXT FEW DAYS, Hattie noticed a change in her mother. She was more agreeable and even weakened on some of her rules.

"You can use your nicknames," Mother told her granddaughters, "but only at home and with school children. If we're at church or other events, you are to use your proper names." She even allowed Hattie to continue wearing her new dresses and restyling her hair. The only one who received her mother's wrath was Josie, insisting to inspect her before she left the house. "No, too fancy for school or too many curls around your face."

If Josie huffed or grimaced and her grandmother caught her, she'd make her change twice, even if she didn't need to. With the younger girls, she'd give them a quick glance and a nod, peck their cheeks, and send them off, which infuriated Josie even more.

Today Josie complained to Hattie. "Why is she so strict with me?"

"It's her way of m-m-making you into a proper young lady." Hattie giggled under her breath, knowing her mother was more concerned about Josie's attitude than her appearance.

"I was doing fine with Mrs. Cushman."

"I'll t-t-talk to her for you," Hattie told Josie. "Better get going before she makes you change again."

Josie grabbed her books and rushed out the door.

"Where's Josie?" Mother asked.

"Already off to s-s-school. She looked fine."

Mother sat in a chair opposite Hattie in the parlor. "She's like breaking a bucking horse."

Hattie laughed. "Yes, that she is, but p-p-perhaps you should ease up a bit."

"Not until I meet Mrs. Cushman and I've extended an invitation twice with no response." She turned to Hattie. "With a spirit like Josie's, you can never show weakness. That's why you've had such trouble with her."

Hattie knew that her mother was right. Mother could size up people within minutes, a trait Hattie admired and wished that she possessed. Hattie always tried to see the good in people, regardless how rude a person might be. Not Mother, she'd respond with a cutting remark right back, but could do it so delicately that it almost seemed like a compliment.

"Hattie," Mother said. "Cecil stopped by earlier. He's heading home next week, after the ball."

Cecil and Mrs. Veysey decided having him gone would make it easier to get Hattie home, saying Mother was too weak to travel on her own.

"Cecil told me that he's leaving," said Hattie. "He's going to ask Margaret Jackson to be his wife. She's a much b-b-better fit than I'd...ever be."

When Mother saw Hattie's relief, she sighed. Guilt overwhelmed her and she suddenly felt ill.

"Mother," said Hattie. "You don't look well. Do you need to rest?"

Mrs. Veysey nodded. She didn't have to pretend to be sick. It was happening on its own. Ever since she had agreed to mislead Hattie, even though she felt she was doing it for Hattie's own good, she had developed stomach cramps and was convinced that it was an ulcer. She also worried if her constitution could handle the deceit, but the worst of it was that she was finding it hard to look Hattie in the eye.

SATURDAY, THE DAY of the ball, the town bustled with excitement. The Veysey Store hung a sign, *Closing at noon.*

Reverend Bradshaw and his wife had agreed to watch Eva and Tillie for the night, so Mrs. Veysey could chaperone Mabs and keep a watchful eye on Josie too. Cecil was also attending, not as Hattie's escort but as a family friend.

At noon, Hattie locked the door and waited five minutes before sneaking out. She had arranged a half-hour session with Professor Wilson, the magic healer. She was eager to see him.

Cloaked in a hooded cape, Hattie hurried up the street to his office and surveyed in both directions before going inside.

Professor Wilson walked out from the back room, mixing a smelly substance in a bowl. "Be with you shortly," he said, and disappeared again.

Excited as Hattie was for another treatment, the professor's approaches scared her, especially when he mentioned the electrical machine. Much as she fretted, she had to admit that all of his methods seemed to help so far.

Suddenly, shouting erupted from behind the long velvet curtain. "Ouch! Dang it! Ouch!!!" Professor Wilson hollered. "Help!"

Hattie leaped up and bolted into the back room. When she saw the professor's sleeve on fire, she dashed over to a water pitcher sitting on a table, hurried back to him with it, and doused him.

He pulled off his coat and smothered the remaining flames with his feet, then pointed to the potbellied stove with a pan atop, sputtering a thick molasses goop onto the floor.

"Oooh," said Hattie, referring to the rancid smell. She grabbed a cloth and pushed the pot off to the side. A few spits hit her sleeve, but didn't penetrate through. She turned back to the professor. "Are you all r-r-right?"

"Yes, yes," he said, wiping his brow with a rag. "My own fault. I shouldn't have turned my back on such a concoction." Hattie crinkled her brow. "A dollop of herbs, spices, and rosemary," he offered, "combined with my secret ingredients to relax the mind. Don't worry, you don't have to drink any."

Hattie gasped when she saw that it was Mrs. Tuttle sitting in the chair sipping a cup of his special remedy.

"She's mesmerized, isn't aware of any of this," he said. "Sure grateful for your help."

"Yes. Of course," said Hattie, staring at the frail woman again, who was now sucking on a cigar and puffing smoke rings into the air without a care.

"She can't know about any of this," he told Hattie. "Otherwise, she'll lose faith in her treatment."

"I see," is all Hattie said, still shocked by what she was witnessing.

"Would you mind assisting me with her?" he asked, wrapping his burnt arm with a bandage. "But I need to swear you to secrecy, patient privacy and all."

Hattie nodded and lifted her hand taking his oath.

"For you to help, I'll need to explain her ailment, but first if you could light another cigar and hand it to me when I tell you." He carefully removed the old cigar from Mrs. Tuttle's hand and extinguished it in a plate.

Mrs. Tuttle clawed the air, reaching for the cigar as if it was in front of her, while her eyes remained shut.

"She's acquired a smoking habit, both cigars and pipes, but through my mesmerizing I've convinced her that if she continues she'll develop man-like traits. And now I'm trying to curb her taste for it too."

"I've n-n-never seen a woman s-s-smoke," said Hattie.

"More common than you think, especially in the larger cities, but she's embarrassed by it." He stepped toward Mrs. Tuttle and spoke in a soothing voice, then turned to Hattie taking the lit cigar from her and placing it in Mrs. Tuttle's hand. "Inhale the smoke and hold it in your mouth. It tastes like cow manure. Do you taste it?" He asked her.

She shook her head.

"Blow it out and take another whiff." After five more tries, she finally said, "yes."

"Spit it out," he commanded, removing the lit cigar and handing it to Hattie to extinguish. He then reached for a pipe, lit it, and slid it into Mrs. Tuttle's mouth. "Yum, yum," he said.

"Delightful," she squealed, puffing on it.

"Tastes like dirty socks," the professor told her.

"No. It's delightful," she repeated.

He looked at Hattie. "The pipe's going to require more sessions. The sweet smell and taste make it a bit harder to trick the senses, but I'll figure it out."

Observing his patience and kindness, Hattie realized he believed in his skill and truly wanted to help people with their ailments. It made her trust him even more.

"Hattie, I'm going to bring her out of her trance, but she can't see you here. Not even in the waiting room." He pointed to a closet. "Please hide in there."

She hurried to the closet and closed the door. After a bit, she heard voices and laughter, then footsteps. The door swung open.

"Appreciate your help," he told her.

"It was f-f-fascinating to watch."

"Let's see how we do with your stuttering."

"Professor, will you be able to cure my stuttering, like Mrs. Tuttle's smoking?"

He frowned. "Wish I could tell you yes, but you're stuttering is a speech impediment caused by nerves. Mrs. Tuttle's is a bad habit, easily broken through hypnosis."

"Oh," she said, staring down at her hands.

"Don't look so defeated. With periodic visits and tricks, we can keep it controlled."

She nodded, but she couldn't shake her disappointment.

"I was thinking today I'd try electrical currents on you. Might have a longer effect."

"El-el-electrical today?"

"Nothing to fret about, it's usually used for relieving pain, but I thought it might put you into a more relaxed form to accept the mesmerizing."

"Okay," said Hattie nervously.

He motioned her to a chair and placed a small wooden box on the table beside her. After he plugged it in and placed the applicator to her neck, a slight vibration shivered down her spine and hummed like a hornet's swarm.

"How you doin?"

"F-f-fine," she said, now noticing her tongue tickling. After what seemed forever, he finally turned off the machine, but the electrical vibration still pulsed in her veins. "I-I-I still feel it."

"Good," he said. "That wasn't so bad, was it?"

Hattie nodded, but her brain disagreed. Not that it hurt, but it felt strange and not something she cared to try again. But she feared that she might have to, to get better.

"Fixes all types of ailments," he claimed. "Most treatments are twenty minutes, but I only used ten minutes on you."

Hattie shuddered from the thought of what ten more minutes would've caused. She was still pulsating and she now worried that it wouldn't stop.

"Now with you relaxed, we can start."

Hattie interrupted. "Professor Wilson, could you *not* have my finger in the air?"

He chuckled when Hattie told him about Mrs. Bailey's observation and the witch remark. "How about I have you pull on your thumb?"

"That would w-w-work," said Hattie.

With this session, he didn't ask if she saw a monkey's tail nor did he have her look at his fingers, but he had her close her eyes tight.

Standing behind her, he placed his hand on her shoulder. "Bees are buzzing around your head, but they won't sting you. Do you hear them?"

She did, but she wasn't sure if it was real or the pulsating still in her from the machine.

"Focus on every buzz," he said.

As she listened, she moved her head in a circle as if she was following the swarm. Professor Wilson whispered into her ear. "Your stuttering will disappear with the pull of your thumb." He repeated the phrase at least ten more times. When he clapped his hands, the buzzing stopped. "Open your eyes," he told her.

He walked to the front of the chair and faced her. "How do you feel?"

She thought a moment. "Energized."

He nodded. "Start talking, but pull on your thumb as you do."

After five long sentences, not one stutter came out. "It worked," she said, jumping out of her seat. "Thank you, Professor." She fished fifty-cents out of her pocket and thanked him two more times.

"No payment today. Grateful for your help with Mrs. Tuttle. Stop by tomorrow and let me know the results."

"Will do," she said, slipping the cape over her shoulders and hurrying out the door.

She raced up the street, but slowed every time a jolt pulsed through her. *Sure hope that goes away.* The professor had explained it was normal and not harmful and would actually energize her even more. Nonetheless, she wished the jolting would stop and definitely not happen in front of Mother.

CHAPTER TWENTY-SEVEN

CECIL HAD RENTED a horse-drawn carriage and purchased a new suit, topcoat, and hat. Hattie had to admit that he looked distinguished and found it appealing that he'd make such an effort for her family.

With white lights strung on the outside banisters, porch beams, and the roof's edge, the Hoquiam Hotel lit up like a giant Christmas tree. Excitement stirred inside of Hattie as their carriage inched forward. There were three carriages ahead and one had just emptied its party at the entry.

"Ekolas just got out of their buggy," remarked Mabs, looking through the binoculars that she had brought. "Now Ivar's stepping out."

"C-c-can I see?" asked Hattie, taking the binoculars from Mabs. "He's so dashing," Hattie whispered. She continued watching as he reached for the white-gloved hand extending out of the carriage. She gawked when she saw a busty woman descend.

"That doesn't look like Josie," Mabs said.

Hattie handed her the binoculars. Disappointment lodged in her gut. "It's Kate, his college friend."

"Uh, oh," said Mabs, watching Josie step out of the carriage next, on the arm of Ivar's seventeen-year-old brother. "Looks like Josie got stuck with good-old Henrik."

Hattie nodded, knowing that it had to have been Kate who orchestrated the switch.

When the Veysey party started up the stairs, Mr. Connell greeted them with a bow and showed them into the lobby. "Wait until you see the ballroom," he said, escorting them down a long hallway.

They entered through double doors into the colossal ballroom. Hattie stared in disbelief at the white-plastered walls, then to the ornate ceiling at least thirty-feet high, and lastly to the jeweled crystal chandelier suspended above the gleaming parquet floors. At the back of the room was the musicians' gallery on a raised landing.

"Over here," Mr. Connell said. "I seated Daphanie and Nora about a half-hour ago," he said, weaving them through lace-covered tables that circled the dance floor to the Marshalls' reserved tables. Mr. Connell turned to Hattie. "Would you like me to take your cape to the cloak room?"

"No. I'm cold," she said, "but thank you."

"See you later," he said, disappearing into the crowd.

Hattie lowered into the chair next to Daphanie. Mabs sat down next to Hattie and fluffed out the lavender gown that Hattie had made for her. Hattie's mother sat next to Mabs and Cecil was on the end.

Nora, on the other side of Daphanie, stood up and stepped over to Hattie. "I feel like a princess. Thank you."

Hattie had redesigned a gold Vaudeville gown to Nora's measurements. Mabs surprised her with it today.

"You're welcome," said Hattie. "You look lovely."

Daphanie turned to Hattie. "Time for us to see your gown, don't you think?"

"I suppose," said Hattie.

Feeling shy, Hattie slowly stood, untied her cape, and removed it. Cecil's mouth popped open as his eyes roved every inch of her. The sapphire-blue gown outlined all of Hattie's curves.

Daphanie grabbed Hattie's hand and pulled her back down to her chair. "You sure fill out that dress nicely."

Hattie blushed. "I didn't know it was s-s-so revealing until I put it on over my corset. I was going to change, but my mother s-s-saw me in it and insisted that I wear it. I should put my cape b-b-back on."

"Don't you dare," said Daphanie. "I'm guessing that your mother wanted Mr. Hickel to see the full package. Might as well let others enjoy it too."

"It's not like that," said Hattie. "Cecil's leaving next week to ask someone else to be his wife. Mother was fine with his decision."

"Really?"

Before Hattie could respond, Mabs interrupted. "Ivar's coming this way."

Daphanie heard a gasp in Hattie's breath and grinned. "Awfully handsome tonight, isn't he?"

Dressed in black tails and slacks, with his thick blond hair combed in place, Ivar was as handsome as Hattie had ever seen him. She also noted all the attention he was drawing from the other young ladies, but his eyes seemed fixed on Hattie.

She blushed and looked away, but when he reached her, she forced herself back to his gaze.

He looked at her anxiously. "May I sit?"

"You can have my chair," Mabs said standing and going to a seat next to Nora.

Ivar's eyes widened. "You're beautiful tonight," he said, sitting down beside her.

"Th-th...." She quickly tugged on her thumb, hoping the Professor's session still worked. "Thank you," she said without a stutter or a jolt.

"Is that your dance card?" he asked, sliding it toward him. "How many dances will you permit me?"

"Aren't you with Kate? Or Josie?"

"I'll throw a few dances their way, but not the slow ones," he said, giving Hattie a grin as he penciled his name into several slow waltzes and two-steps. He leaned toward her. "Those are for you."

Hattie gulped and her heart raced erratically. She didn't see Leona Marshall until she tapped Hattie on the shoulder. "So glad you made it. Again, I'm so sorry about the hats."

"It all worked out," said Hattie.

"I've received so many compliments on my gown," said Leona. She hugged Hattie. "And you made it happen." She whispered into Hattie's ear. "You're breathtaking tonight and he's the catch of this ball. Have a delightful evening."

THE BALL STARTED with a Grand March to *Stars and Stripes Forever.* It was the first time tonight that Hattie had seen Josie up close. She looked lovely in her copper-toned gown.

After the marching stopped, the music commenced into a waltz. Ivar walked over and extended his hand to Hattie, helping her out of the chair. Once he placed his hands on her waist, he gently moved her across the floor to the *Skaters Waltz*. "One of my favorite tunes," he said.

"It is lovely," Hattie said, smiling. The next dance was a two-step to *Pop Goes the Weasel*. They laughed as much as they danced.

Listening to another waltz, Ivar escorted her to the middle of the floor. "What a perfect song," he said.

"What is it?"

"Johann Strauss' *Vienna Waltz*. For the pretty girl I'm dancing with." Hattie blushed. Blushing around Ivar had become a common occurrence. He clasped one hand into Hattie's and gently placed his other against her back. Moving across the floor, Ivar studied her face. Whenever Hattie brought her gaze back to his, he smiled and stared intently. Her stomach fluttered and she easily followed as he guided them across the floor. She was in pure heaven and didn't want the music to stop. For that moment, it was just her and him on the dance floor, until Cecil tapped his finger on Ivar's shoulder.

"Cutting in," Cecil said.

Slightly annoyed, Ivar handed Hattie to Cecil. Walking away, Ivar was met by Kate who pulled him back out to the floor. Hattie's heart sank as she watched. She tried not to show her displeasure of Cecil interrupting her dance with Ivar, until he tightened his arms around her.

Moving her slowly in circles, he pressed against her. She fidgeted. "Cecil, you're holding me too tight."

"Didn't seem to bother you with that other guy."

"Stop it," she whispered. "You're embarrassing me. Margaret wouldn't approve."

He glared at her. "Think I care about that old hag when I got you?" She got a whiff of his breath and realized that he'd been drinking. *He must have a flask on him.* "From now on, no one holds you but me," he said, pulling her even closer.

Startled by his controlling attitude, she stomped on his foot and squirmed herself loose. When she turned, she saw Bert coming toward her. She rushed to him and wrapped her arms around him. "Bert, how wonderful to see you."

"Don't you look the sight," he said, eyeing Cecil as he staggered across the floor and out the door. "Who's the man you were dancing with?"

Hattie shook her head. "A family friend."

She was still fuming over Cecil's behavior, but seeing Bert erased most of her anger. "I didn't think I'd ever see you out of the cookhouse." She grabbed his hand and pulled him over to her table. After Hattie introduced him, Bert sat down next to her. She glanced over to where Cecil had been sitting and was relieved to find him still gone. At intermission, the ballroom grew noisy as groups gathered.

"I'll be back," Bert told Hattie, leaving an empty seat next to her.

Hattie watched with interest as Bert wandered over to the Ekola table. He patted Ivar on the back, the two talked for a minute, and then Bert sat down next to Ivar's parents. She was hoping that Ivar would make his way over to her, but he seemed preoccupied with his group. And it appeared even if he wanted to leave, he was trapped.

Kate glanced over several times, and when she caught Hattie looking back, she wrapped her arms around Ivar and kissed his cheek. It caught his attention, and a moment later, the two were talking and laughing.

Hattie sighed. *Who am I fooling? He's wedged in Kate's web and Ivar's mother is helping with the weaving.* She flinched when she felt a hand touch her shoulder and spun around expecting Cecil. Instead, it was Nick Cooper, her logger friend from the camp.

"Remember me?" he said. He wasn't dressed as suave as Ivar, or Cecil for that matter, but he looked awfully nice in his black slacks, matching jacket, and white shirt.

Daphanie's eyebrows shot up.

"May I have the next dance?" he asked.

"Yes," said Hattie nervously. "It's wonderful to see you. Did you come with B-B-Bert?" She pulled on her thumb to stop her stuttering, but it wasn't working. She had forgotten the effect that this handsome logger had on her. With Ivar her heart would flutter, but whenever Nick came near something else stirred—maybe his poetry and his stories. She wasn't sure.

"Yes, I rode in with Bert." He was taking her in the same way that Cecil did, but for some reason Hattie didn't mind his roving eyes. When she glanced over at her mother, she got a disapproving stare.

"And who are you?" Daphanie inquired. "Certainly aren't a regular in these parts. I would've noticed."

When he grinned, showing his perfect smile, Hattie was certain that Daphanie swooned a bit, but so did Hattie, silently.

"I'm Nick. I work at the Ekola camp," he told her.

"Oh, Nick," said Daphanie, nodding.

Another waltz started up. Nick extended his arm to Hattie and led her out to the floor. He gently cupped his hand in the small of her back. She shivered from his touch. Gliding her across the floor, his steps were even smoother than Ivar's.

"You're a good d-d-dancer," said Hattie.

"Another skill my mother insisted on," he told her. Proper dancing. You're good too."

"No," she said. "Daphanie's been t-t-teaching me all week. I only really know folk-dance steps."

"No worries. It's the man who leads," he said. "You're doing fine." He pulled her close and twirled her across the floor. When she straightened her gaze, she saw Ivar staring. He started to get up from his chair, but Kate grabbed onto his arm.

The music stopped. "Hattie," Nick said, "could we sit in the lobby and visit?"

Hattie nodded. On their way to the lobby, they passed the Ekola table. Hattie caught Ivar's glance again. He looked at her in disbelief, but not shocked enough to remove Kate's hand from his neck.

Josie gawked too. "Who's that with Hattie?" she asked loud enough for everyone to hear.

IN A PRIVATE CORNER, Nick sat beside Hattie on a sofa. "Never thought I'd see you again," he said.

"It's a surprise to s-s-see you too."

"Hope it's a nice surprise," he added.

"Very much," she admitted, her heart thumping erratically.

"Who was that lug pawing you on the dance floor?"

Hattie sighed. "An old f-f-family friend. He escorted my mother out from Wisconsin."

"By the looks of it, he has a strong interest in you. Can't say that I blame him. You're as lovely as an orchid."

Hattie felt her cheeks redden and looked toward the floor. She pulled on her thumb, hoping to control her stuttering. "Our parents were trying to f-f-fix us up, but as soon as he returns home, he's asking another girl to m-m-marry him."

"Be careful, Hattie. That man might say he's chosen someone else, but he was holding you too possessive, like he owned you."

"I believe he'd been drinking."

"That's worse," said Nick. "That's when a man's true colors show. Trust me, he wants you for himself. You're too good for a man like that."

Hattie wondered if he might be talking about himself. Nick had made it clear at the logging camp that he was not the settling-down type. It seemed that he still had so many adventures ahead. Nonetheless, she couldn't help but be flattered by his attention; especially after Ivar had dismissed her at the camp. Nick, always a gentleman, never pursued her, not even for a kiss.

He reached into his pocket. "I wrote you a sonnet titled *Inspired Beauty*. May I read it to you?"

"Y-y-yes," she said, feeling her face redden.

He smiled and cleared his throat.

"*Your retreating essence beholds emblems of precious stems. Swirling petals and enticing panicles simply pure and lusted. You're an heirloom bursting into a Sunkist blossom.*"

Nick had told her that poetry was full of abstract meaning. She was captured by his words and was so riveted by them that her head was spinning. "That was b-b-beautiful."

"It has a hidden meaning," he said.

"Oh. What is it?"

"That's for you to decipher." He handed her the sonnet and casually leaned back, his long legs stretched in front of him. "What's the story between you and Ekola?"

"Ivar? We're just friends."

"Didn't look that way to me."

"Not sure what you mean," she said.

"The way he was gazing into your eyes, there was something more. Bert commented on it too. I got a twinge of jealousy when I saw you two together."

Hattie gave him a puzzled stare.

"Are you stuck on him?"

Hattie shrugged her shoulders.

Nick leaped to his feet and pulled Hattie with him. "Only one way to find out." He wrapped his arms around her. Before she realized what was happening, Nick pressed his mouth softly to hers. As his kiss lingered, heat rushed through her and whisked her into his tender embrace. Suddenly, a hand landed on Nick's shoulder and jerked him back. Just as Nick spun around, Ivar punched him in the jaw, forcing him to the ground.

Hattie's hand flew over her mouth.

Ivar darted his eyes to Nick still on the floor and then back to Hattie with a disgraced expression on his face. She wasn't sure if it was meant for her or that he was shameful for what had just happened. Shaking his head, he muttered under his breath and brushed past her.

Rubbing his chin, Nick looked up at her and winked. "Think we got an answer," he said, standing.

Stupefied by it all, Hattie stood motionless. Her emotions flooded with anger, hurt, embarrassment, all wrapped into one. Tears welled in her eyes.

"Did you kiss me just to get Ivar's reaction?"

"Partly, but I wanted your reaction too. I'm sorry. I didn't mean to hurt you."

When she heard the hum of a crowd behind her, she glanced over her shoulder and gasped. Mother, Josie, Kate, Mrs. Cushman, and Mrs. Ekola were all ogling with judgmental stares, as other onlookers blurred before her. Mortified, she raced to the door.

Nick resisted chasing after her. He had come to tell her how he felt and hoped she'd give him a chance. *What was I thinking? She belongs to him.*

Bert walked up. "Seems you got into a bit of a scuffle. Sorry to say, I may have pushed it."

"It was bound to happen," Nick said.

"You care about Hattie, don't you?"

He sighed and nodded. "She consumes my every thought. Wish she didn't, but she does."

"She's a rare mold," Bert said.

"Does Ekola realize how lucky he is?"

Bert slapped Nick on the back. "Don't know. He might be fool enough not to, until it's too late."

"I understand that," said Nick.

DAPHANIE AND MABS found Hattie sitting on a far bench, holding a hankie to her face. She looked up at them as they sat beside her. She broke into tears again. "How did this all h-h-happen?"

"I can explain it," said Mabs. "I was sitting at the Ekola table, next to Josie."

"Spill it," said Daphanie. "You got my curiosity."

"It started with Ivar and Bert sparing back and forth with joking words," said Mabs. "When Ivar saw Hattie dancing with Nick, he turned on Bert demanding answers."

Hattie slowly exhaled a deep breath. "It was really q-q-quite innocent."

"Ivar didn't see it that way," said Mabs. "He pressed until Bert got mad and told Ivar that Nick probably just came for another kiss. That's when Ivar leaped out of his chair like a wild bear. Kate grabbed for his sleeve, trying to stop him, but he yanked it out of her hand and stormed toward the lobby."

Daphanie nodded to Hattie. "We saw the ruckus from our table, but it wasn't until Henrik hollered *fight* and chased after his brother that I knew it had to do with you. Mabs confirmed it when she raced out. Your mother caught on too."

Hattie sighed.

Daphanie wrinkled her brow. "So, why did Ivar hit him if you were just talking?"

Hattie sheepishly looked at her.

"I see," she said. "You were kissing."

"Yes...no. I mean...everything happened so fast."

CHAPTER TWENTY-EIGHT

WHEN THE CONDUCTOR gave final call, Mother motioned to Hattie. "Come along."

Mother insisted that Hattie head back to Wisconsin with Cecil and she would stay behind with the girls. "News of the fight has spread through town and causing too much embarrassment for the store," Mother had told her. What she didn't add was that this incident was the force needed to get Hattie back to Wisconsin and she was relieved that it didn't require any tricks on her part. She was already wrenched with guilt and not sure how much more her stomach could handle.

Hattie had already said goodbye to Daphanie, Mr. Connell, and to all of her other friends too. Cecil had arranged for Hattie's trunk to be picked up last night and would be meeting them at the station.

The girls had agreed not to accompany Hattie to the train. "I'll write the moment I reach Wisconsin," she had told them. Tillie had fussed the most. Eva sulked and hugged Hattie longer than the others. Mabs' eyes filled with tears as she promised to visit Wisconsin next year. Josie didn't come to say goodbye. Hattie hadn't seen her in the three days since the ball and wasn't upset with her absence. Mother didn't question Josie's nonappearance either. Mabs reported that Ivar had headed back to the university with Kate. Hattie's heart ached from that news, but she realized that once Kate had claimed him for her own that was that.

"Have a good trip," Mother said. "You know this is for the best."

Feeling too deflated to argue, Hattie nodded. She wasn't sure how she felt about going back to the farm. Seeing Wallace would be wonderful, but the rest of it hadn't sunk in.

"Plus it will give you and Cecil a chance to reacquaint," Mother added. "Emotions might harvest on such a long journey."

"He's marrying Margaret, Mother."

"Just be open to it, please?"

Hattie sighed.

"Shouldn't be more than a few more weeks before Leon and Mary return, and then I'll be home."

Cecil, already on the train, tapped on the window and mouthed, "Time to go."

Hattie hugged her mother, turned, and boarded.

THE TRAIN CHUGGED from the station and she wept into her hankie, already missing everyone. Cecil wrapped his arm around her. "Hattie," he whispered. "After all that has happened, it's right that you're heading home with me."

She looked at him through tearful eyes, and before she could answer, he leaned down and kissed her. When he kissed her more aggressively, she pushed on his chest until he released her. It reminded her of how he had acted at the ball. "Stop," she told him. "Please." She scooted over to the window, lifted her carpetbag from the floor, and placed it between them. Then she turned toward the window, rested her head against the seat, and closed her eyes.

Cecil chuckled under his breath. "Think that little bag is going to keep me away?"

When she didn't answer, he settled back into his seat. Hattie struggled with worry, thinking back to what Nick had observed: that Cecil was too possessive, as if he owned her. She shivered from the thought. She was angry that she had agreed to travel home with him.

When Cecil reached over and started rubbing her back, she twisted upright and turned her head. "Cecil, s-s-stop it. Think of Margaret."

He furrowed his brow. "Margaret?"

"Your f-f-future bride. I'm sure she wouldn't approve. You're out of line."

"You didn't seem to mind when I kissed you."

"You caught me off g-g-guard."

"We'll talk after you're better rested," he said.

"About what?"

"Us."

She wanted to yell, *there is no us*, but decided it was easier for now to let it go. She realized too that she needed to redirect his thinking back to Margaret. One thing that was certain, she wasn't going to put up with his advances for five more days.

THREE HOURS LATER they reached the Tacoma Depot. On her initial trip to Hoquiam, the train had bypassed this stop and she was grateful to be seeing this magnificent structure now with its tall ceramic arches everywhere she looked. This would be a two-hour layover to load more passengers heading east.

"It will be good to get off," said Cecil, yawning loud enough for people to look. "Are you hungry?"

"Yes," said Hattie, grabbing her carpetbag.

"You can leave that here," he said. "It will be safe."

"No, I like h-h-having it with me."

She followed Cecil to the aisle. He insisted that she go first, but didn't give way for her to get by him comfortably. Instead, she had to squeeze close to him. It annoyed Hattie beyond words.

Stepping off the train, Hattie noted the park-like setting of the indoor domed building: benches, tall plants and trees, and food carts littered throughout. All that was missing were ducks in a pond.

"I w-w-wonder where all these people are going?" Hattie said. "It's fascinating to imagine."

"Sounds like you find travel exciting," said Cecil.

"Yes, don't you?"

"I've done it so much, it seems drab. But if it's something that would add spark for you, we'd go anytime and anywhere time permitting." He reached for her bag, and with his other arm, looped it around her waist. "Stay close, don't want to lose you."

Hattie didn't fight him. There were so many people bumping into them and rushing past them, it almost made her dizzy. Having Cecil guide her brought her relief from all of the confusion.

"It's good to have me as a protector, isn't it?"

"Yes," she admitted. She just wished he wasn't using

it as an opportunity to hold her closer than necessary.

"This way," he said, heading them to an eatery.

Hattie caught her breath and studied the new surroundings. Instead of chairs, there were padded bench-like sofas on each side of a shared table.

"They're called booths," said Cecil, placing Hattie's bag on the opposite side of where she was sitting, before he plopped down and scooted close to her, trapping her against the wall.

Placing her napkin in her lap, she elbowed Cecil in the side, hoping he'd get the hint to move over. Instead, he put his arm around the top of the bench and extended it behind her to where his hand touched her far shoulder.

"How am I s-s-supposed to eat with you so near?"

"Food isn't here yet," he said, smiling devilishly.

After they finished their meal, Cecil was on his second whiskey. Hattie didn't care for his slurring, but what really annoyed her were his traveling fingers stroking her neck, then her back, and her cheek. The more she opposed, the more he persisted.

"Should we get back to the train?" said Hattie.

He looked at his pocket watch. "No reason to leave, we still have an hour. You sure I can't get you something to drink? It might relax you." She shook her head. He stood up and stretched. "I need to use the privy. Be right back."

Hattie watched as he weaved to the front counter and disappeared. When the waiter returned and asked if she needed anything else, she answered, "Yes, please tell the gentleman that I headed back to the train."

"Will do," he said.

She scooted off the bench, reached for her carpetbag, and disappeared out the side door to the eastbound trains. Thinking once she approached, she'd recognize her train, but multiple ones with long Pullmans and steam snorting from their engines lined the tracks. One by one, she found the porter and inquired the destination. After four trains and four inquiries, she finally located it. Passing under the windows toward the door, she spotted Cecil's bowler hat sitting atop his carry-on. She sighed. *With a belly full of whiskey, he's going to be a handful.* She saw no need to get on early, especially if he hurried back, so she headed to a bench beyond the engine and sat down. A thin young woman with long brown hair walked up, nodded to Hattie, and sat on the opposite end of the bench.

"Hello," she said. "Where are you headed?" The young woman, more plain than pretty, had a wholesome oblong face and a nice smile with a bit of an overbite.

"Wisconsin," Hattie answered.

"I just saw my brother off to New York. Thought I'd give my feet a rest before walking back home."

As the two talked, Hattie learned that the young woman, now twenty-four, had accompanied her older sister from New York three years ago. Her sister had secured a teaching position in Tacoma, and Ella, the young woman, was to stay until her sister had settled in.

"W-w-what happened?" asked Hattie.

"Within six months, she got married, and a month later, a baby was on the way. I moved to a nearby boarding house to help her with her new life. After a while, I liked being on my own and saw no reason to leave. I work at the drug store and get by just fine. What about you?"

"I came out to h-h-help in my brother's mercantile," said Hattie, "and to care for my younger n-n-nieces, but now I'm going back to the farm."

"What do you do on the farm?" asked Ella.

"I'm a dairymaid," she said.

"A dairymaid?"

"Milk cows, feed them, and clean their stalls. I do b-b-bookkeeping and cooking too." She paused. "And I suppose one day will marry." As she said it aloud, she realized how unappealing it sounded, especially the marriage part. More than likely her mother would push her to Cecil, and with his persistence, the two would wear her down. "Wish I had a b-b-boarding house to go to."

"You can board at mine. There's rooms available at winter rates. Only three dollars a week."

Hattie shook her head. "It'd be too disruptive."

"To who?"

Just as Ella asked, Hattie spotted Cecil stumbling aboard the train. Her anger grew from the sight. She turned back to Ella. "You have no idea how I wish I didn't have to get b-b-back on that train."

"So why go?"

Hattie looked toward the train again. She pondered for a moment, then looked down at Ella. "I could rent weekly?"

"Yes," said Ella.

"Hmm."

Rationalizing the idea, she was tempted, but she was scared too. She stood. "It was nice meeting you."

"You too," the young woman said.

The closer Hattie got to the train, the more her anxiety grew until a sudden urge to run pulsed through her. She stopped. *Why not? I have forty dollars and a change of clothes.* She quickly turned around and raced back to Ella.

CHAPTER TWENTY-NINE

MILLIE'S BOARDING HOUSE with views of Puget Sound looked like a cottage in a seascape painting: weathered-gray shingles, a dark blue door with matching shutters on the windows, and baskets with lush green ferns hanging from a long open porch.

"Here we are," said Ella, leading Hattie through the door. "Millie," she called out.

A stout gray-haired woman with a wrinkled face and twinkling eyes walked out from the kitchen, rubbing her hands on her apron. "Yaa," she said in a strong German accent.

"This is Hattie. She wants to rent a room."

Millie nodded and gave Hattie a quick look over. "Three dollars, up front." Hattie reached into her coat pocket and handed her the money. Millie turned to Ella. "She can have the room next to you. Supper in an hour. Hope you like franks and sauerkraut. Apple strudel for dessert."

BY THE THIRD day, Hattie had settled in. Her small room was sparse but efficient with a double bed, a single dresser, and small stand, which held a water pitcher. She shared the upstairs privy with two others. Breakfast and dinner were served at specific times: eight a.m. and five o'clock, in a formal dining room with proper table settings including a lace tablecloth.

Once Millie discovered that Hattie stuttered, she limited asking her detailed questions during meals but probed for more if she caught her alone in the kitchen or the parlor. At first, Hattie didn't like her prying, but knew she'd have to furnish some information. It actually surprised Hattie how well she had mastered telling her just enough to satisfy her curiosity, but not more that would require further explanation.

After breakfast, Hattie walked along Puget Sound, smelling the salt air and listening to the seagulls. It gave her time to think, but most of those thoughts traveled back to Hoquiam. She longed to see Ivar, to explain. At the ball, he showed a glimpse of interest, until Nick showed up. Nick? Her stomach tightened. What has become of you? She liked him, liked him a lot, but she knew he was too much of a drifter for her to contemplate thoughts. Maybe Ivar was too. Just in a different way.

She spotted the telegraph office on the next block and headed to it. She wrote out a simple message to her brother Wallace in Wisconsin.

Handing it to the clerk, she sighed from knowing that her news of leaving the train would soon be known all around town. The clerk at the Waupaca telegraph office always tried to be discreet, but if something provoked his interest, he couldn't resist spreading it. She just prayed that he'd wait until Wallace read the message first. And if Wallace ran into Cecil, she knew he'd hear an earful from him too.

Oh well, not the first time I've become a spectacle. At least I'm not there to witness it.

> **WESTERN UNION TELEGRAM**
>
> Transmitted From: Tacoma, WA 11/07/1903 1:00 p.m.
> Received At: Waupaca, WI
>
> WALLACE-
> PICK UP MY TRUNK AT WAUPACA STATION. IT'S ARRIVING IN TWO DAYS. I GOT OFF TRAIN IN TACOMA. WILL SEND LETTER.
>
> HATTIE

"Is there a p-p-public telephone?" she asked the telegraph clerk.

The clerk pointed to a wooden box bolted to the opposite wall. "Local calls under three minutes cost twenty cents. You pay me here."

"Mine will be long d-d-distance to Montesano."

He looked at a chart and quoted her forty cents. "Try to keep it short, long distance adds up fast. The operator will call back if you exceed three minutes."

She placed the money on the counter and walked over to the telephone. Holding the earpiece to her ear, she cranked the telephone, and then spoke into the long tube mouthpiece.

"Veysey Store," a man's voice said.

"Is Charles there?" Her voice trembled. "This is his s-s-sister, Hattie."

"Just a minute." It seemed more than one minute before Charles reached the phone.

"Hattie?"

"I'm calling from T-T-Tacoma, can't talk long."

"Tacoma?"

"I got off the t-t-train. I'm staying at Millie's Boarding House. I just n-n-needed to think."

"I don't understand. Did something happen?"

Hattie paused, choking back tears. "No."

"Do you want me to come get you?"

"No."

"Do you need money? I could telegraph some."

"I h-h-have enough for now and I'm going to cash out the t-t-train ticket. Give me another w-w-week to figure things out."

The operator interrupted, "three minutes."

"Charles, p-p-please tell Mother I'm sorry. We'll talk next week. I have to go." *Click.*

BY THE FOLLOWING Wednesday, Hattie had been in Tacoma for eight days. During that time, she had called Charles twice, reported that she was fine and enjoyed being on her own, and that she might even look for work. When she inquired about Mother, he replied, "Don't worry, I'm handling it."

Hattie appreciated that her brother didn't press for answers. He only listened and told her to call anytime. Her letter to Wallace briefly outlined the events: the hat fiasco, the fight at the ball, and Cecil's persistence with marriage. Of course, she knew if Wallace asked Cecil if he had pressured her, he'd deny it and state it was all in Hattie's head.

Ella knocked at the door and talked through it. "You have visitors in the parlor."

"Thank you, Ella. I'll be right down."

Hattie checked herself in the mirror, took a deep breath, and headed to the stairs.

"Charles," said Hattie, her voice quivered. She scanned the room for her mother. Instead, she saw a pretty woman with a welcoming smile.

Charles hugged Hattie. "So good to see you," and then walked her over to his new wife Nettie, and introduced her. "I've tried to keep calm about you being on your own," he added, "but I couldn't hold off any longer."

"I'm h-h-happy to see you," said Hattie. She turned to Nettie again, "and to finally m-m-meet you."

"As am I," said Nettie.

"We're staying at a resort up the street," said Charles. "It has a nice dining room overlooking Puget Sound. Thought you might join us for a bite to eat."

"I'd like that," said Hattie. "Let me tell Millie so she doesn't fix me a plate tonight. Be right back."

Nettie waited until Hattie was out of earshot. "I'm too excited," she told her husband. "Tell her now."

Charles looked at his wife and shook his head. "Before we drop something else in her lap, I think it might be best for us to learn why she got off the train."

"Of course, dear," agreed Nettie, "but this news will put a positive start to our visit, instead of her dreading it. I'm sure she's nervous to talk to you."

"All set," said Hattie, walking into the parlor.

"Take a seat, please," Charles said. "I have something to show you." He pulled a newspaper clipping out of his pocket and handed it to Hattie.

THE WASHINGTONIAN
November 10, 1903

HOQUIAM
GOVERNOR'S RECEPTION

LOCAL GIRL, WITH HELP OF TOWNSPEOPLE, MAKES A CHARITABLE EVENT A SUCCESS!

After a hat order had been lost and another one partially destroyed, hats were donated by local women and redesigned by Miss Hattie Veysey of the Veysey Mercantile. All proceeds went to the victims of the Aberdeen fire.

Pictured wearing one of the hats is the Governor's wife, Mrs. McBride, and Mrs. Gerald Cushman, the reception organizer. Mrs. McBride claimed that this hat was one of the loveliest she has ever worn and plans to make it a wardrobe staple.

After reading the article, Hattie glanced up. "How?" She looked down at the picture attached and studied it before speaking again. "Is th-th-that Mrs. Cushman?"

"Yes," answered Charles, "with Mrs. McBride, the governor's wife."

Hattie gasped, re-examining the article and the picture again.

In the picture taken at the reception, both women were wearing one of Hattie's redesigned fancy hats. Hattie looked at her brother again. "This is h-h-hard to believe. How did it all happen?"

"It started after Mr. Connell wrote a human-interest story for the newspaper and displayed your hats in the Economy Store window."

Charles placed Mr. Connell's article into Hattie's lap and continued talking. "After Mrs. McBride read his story, she sent her assistant to the Economy Store to buy one of your hats."

"I still c-c-can't believe it."

Charles explained that Mrs. McBride's assistant, a stark businessman in a three-piece suit, had brought a reporter and photographer along.

"A picture of him buying your hat for the governor's wife appeared in the newspaper next day and caused a rush. Your hats sold out within hours."

"Oh, my," said Hattie.

"The hat has become famous whenever the governor's wife wears it." He pulled another paper out of his pocket. "You have twenty-five pending orders to fill.

And yesterday I got a call from a San Francisco department store wanting to hire you for special orders."

Speechless, Hattie froze.

"You don't have to say anything now," Charles said, "but we have a proposal. You set up shop in the Aberdeen store and take the upstairs living quarters."

Not sure if she was hearing her brother correctly, she shook her head. "Are you s-s-suggesting I open up a business?"

"Yep."

"What about your g-g-grocery store and your home?"

"With all the rebuilding after the fire, a larger grocer is going in on the next block. Honestly, I wasn't sure what to do with Aberdeen."

Hattie slumped back in the chair.

"I've wanted to expand in Montesano for a long time," said Charles, "and we just put an offer on a house there near Nettie's parents. Aberdeen would be a perfect setup for a millinery."

Figure 12
(Courtesy of the Veysey Family Collection)

CHAPTER THIRTY

THE TALL POST with a large letter-shaped *V* attached stood outside on the sidewalk, the same as the one in Hoquiam did. Except this one spelled HATTIE'S on one side of the giant *V* sign, and the other side advertised MILLINERY. Her business name, painted in white on her storefront window, did the same:

HATTIE'S MILLINERY

Hattie, now settled in Charles and Nettie's old living quarters above the Aberdeen store, was making all types of hats. She even catered to the ladies in the brothels, who lived less than two blocks away. With Hoquiam only a thirty-minute streetcar ride from Aberdeen, she had frequent visits with her family and others, plus sessions with the Magic Healer. Mary and Leon, now home from quarantine, were added support.

Mother stayed through the holidays, and after Wallace had written that Cecil eloped with Margaret, Mother didn't pressure Hattie to return to Wisconsin. The only news of Ivar was that he was seen in town escorting another pretty gal.

WHEN THE TINY BELL dinged, Hattie put down her needle and thread, and walked to the front of the store. She gasped at the same time that he did, her heart now pounding up to her throat. She had thought of him, but never dreamed she'd see him again.

"It is you," Nick said, shaking his head. "I couldn't believe it when I passed the window and saw you inside. How have you been, Hattie?"

"Fine."

There was an awkward silence between them.

"Please forgive me. After the scuffle, I came to your store to apologize, but was told you had left that morning by train. Broke my heart when I heard."

Wringing her hands like a nervous child, Hattie gave him a wobbly grin and nodded.

He scanned the room. "Is this your business?"

"Yes, I make h-h-hats."

"I'll be." He walked over to a display table. "These are meticulous," he commented, looking at the flamboyant hats with peacock feathers and subtle-colored plumes. "You never mentioned such a talent."

"It all h-h-happened by accident," she said. "Remember when you t-t-told me that poetry captured your soul?"

"Yes."

"That's the way I feel about m-m-my hats. This used to be my brother's...grocery and dry goods. He moved to Montesano to expand the b-b-business...and offered me th-th-this location." She was stretching her sentences to minimize her stuttering, but found that she was more nervous than normal.

"That's great. I would like to get a hat for my aunt. She lost everything in the fire."

"I'll make one for her. What's your aunt's favorite c-c-color?"

"Blue, I think."

"Are you s-s-still at the logging camp?" she asked.

"No," he said, giving her a sheepish grin. "After the incident, I came to Aberdeen to stay with relatives and got hired as a foreman in the shipyard. On my days off, I'm rebuilding my uncle's jewelry store. It was burnt to the ground. It's two blocks from here."

It was obvious to Hattie that Nick had just come from work. He was wearing a blue flannel shirt, denim pants, and logger-type boots. He was in need of a shave, but the dark stubble pricking across his jaw made him ruggedly handsome. When a strand of his thick dark hair fell across his forehead, he raked it back with his fingers.

Seeming nervous to be standing in front of her now, he cleared his throat. "Look, I'm going to cut right to it. I came to the dance that night to tell you how I felt. And I kissed you to see if you had any feelings for me." He sighed. "But deep down, I knew your heart belonged to him. That's why I didn't come after you."

Hattie's hand flew over her mouth. Tears started welling in her eyes.

"I'll stop by next week to place the order."

"Okay. I'll pull some s-s-samples together."

Watching him walk away, her stomach wrenched and buried emotions flooded through her. She loved when he read poetry to her, and when he told her about little Becca, a part of her fell in love with him that night. However, as magnetized as she was to him, she also knew he was a drifter. She convinced herself instead that it was Ivar who had won her heart, but she had come to realize that Ivar was too fickle and easily swayed, and needed some growing up. Just as Nick reached for the door, she hollered, "I would have chosen you."

He turned around. "What did you say?"

She took a deep breath and walked toward him. "When you k-k-kissed me, feelings unleashed that I didn't know...I had."

His mouth popped open. "For me?" he said in a questioning tone. "You had feelings for me, not him?"

She nodded.

He stood motionless staring at her.

"I made beef stew last n-n-night. If you'd like to join me, I can lock up now and get it warmed."

His smile broadened into a dangerous grin. "Let me help." Heading to the door, he locked it, pulled down all of the shades, and walked back to her.

Hattie shivered from his closeness. "You can light the upstairs p-p-potbelly stove," she said, her voice now quavering, "and I'll be up in a minute."

"Something I need to do first," he said. He pulled her into his arms and gently kissed her. "Hattie," he whispered. "I never knew how lonely I was until I lost you."

When he heard a catch in her breath, he pressed his mouth hard against hers, and with hungry lips, wandered to her neck, and then back to her mouth. His warm taste made her woozy. A moan quivered from her lips, pulsing his breathing out of control.

His lips feverously traveled to her throat again, and then up to her ear, his voice husky. "You're my sonnet, my everlasting poem. I love you, Hattie."

Heat raged through her, her heart thumping with fragmented beats. "Oh, Nick," she gasped, swallowing a breath. "I love you too." Her lips swayed softly against his as tears spilled down her cheeks.

He drew back, his eyes lovingly absorbing her face. "Why are you crying?"

"I'm afraid you'll change your m-m-mind."

His face sobered. "Why would you think that?"

"My st-st-stuttering. It may overwhelm you. And you m-m-might become embarrassed by me."

With his finger, he traced the edge of her chin. "That will never happen." His eyes steady on hers. "You believe me, don't you?"

"I want to."

He gently kissed her again, and then pressed his forehead against hers. "Your stuttering is like a wild primrose, sun shining on all its imperfections as it surrenders to Nature's beauty."

"What lovely w-w-words. Whose are they?"

"Mine." He gazed into her eyes and stroked her cheek. "I love everything about you, Hattie, including your stutter, and I always will." He pulled the ring off his finger and slid it onto hers.

"Becca's ring?"

"It's yours now. I don't need old memories when I have a lifetime to make new ones with you. Will you be my ever-after?" She nodded and melted into his arms.

RESOURCES

Washington, West of the Cascades by Herbert Hunt Volume 3, S. J. Clarke Publishing Company, Published 1917 (Pages 398-399).

They tried to cut it all, Edwin Van Syckle, Published by Craftsman Press, Seattle, WA 1980, (Page 4 – dreaded signal), (Chapter 3 Life in the Camps, Pg 54-80: camp cook, gut hammer, flunkies, Shindig, tin pants, etc.)

The River Pioneers-Early Days on Grays Harbor, Edwin Van Syckle, Published by Pacific Search Press, Seattle, WA 1982, (Pages 235-241) October 16, 1903 Black Friday Fire, Aberdeen, Washington.

School Days, 1970, by Clara Knack. (Description of Hoquiam in 1898, plus references to the Economy Store and Mastin and Nettie Taylor.)

On the Harbor, From Black Friday to Nirvana by John Hughes & Ryan Teague Beckwith, Stephens Press, Las Vegas, published 2005, 2012 (Pg 4-13).

Photo permissions received from *The University of Washington Libraries, Special Collections* and the *Jones Photo Collection*. Other photos and articles were family-owned collections.

AUTHOR'S NOTE

Author KB Taylor is a Veysey descendent

THE VEYSEY BROS: (pronounced: Vee-cee)

1886, CHARLES F. VEYSEY traveled west from Wisconsin to scout out opportunities. His brother MARION later joined him.

1892, he and Marion started the Montesano mercantile, selling sewing machines and later adding groceries. Their brother WALLACE joined them for a short time, but returned to farming.

1902, youngest brother LEON arrived with his family to manage the Hoquiam store. He later became president, relocated to Montesano, and expanded to three stores there. By 1923, Veysey Bros. was one of the largest businesses in Montesano.

1903, Charles married his second wife Nettie Shelley, daughter of R.L Shelley, one-time mayor of Montesano.

October 16, 1903, a massive fire spread throughout Aberdeen's business section. The Veysey Store was one of the few still intact after the fire. Reference: Jones Collection photos (45448-1 and 4339-1).

Page 12 of *On the Harbor, From Black Friday to Nirvana*, referenced the following from a newspaper article: [2]

Charles Veysey, who owned a clothing and grocery store on the northern side of Heron, offered free groceries to anyone left without food and shelter.

1905, Charles and Marion incorporated Veysey Bros., and in October of that same year, Marion suddenly died.

1907, Charles ran for Washington State Senate, but did not win.

1910, all the stores except for Montesano had been closed. With brother Leon now president and part owner, Charles retired in Eagle Rock, near Pasadena, California.

HATTIE J. VEYSEY, youngest child of five and the only girl, visited Grays Harbor in 1903 and again in 1905 for her brother Marion's funeral. Their father while visiting Aberdeen died two months later. During this time, Hattie assisted in all of the stores. Family records reveal that Hattie stammered as a young girl. Stammering was not foreign to the author. Her paternal grandfather

---

[2] *On the Harbor, From Black Friday to Nirvana* by John C. Hughes and Ryan Teague Beckwith, Stephens Press LLC, Las Vegas, published 2005 and 2012.

stammered. She knew to be patient, let him finish his words, and never try to insert one for him. He never let his stuttering define him.

THE ECONOMY STORE also listed as the Temple of Economy was owned by Great-Grandparents Mastin and Nettie Connell Taylor. It was fourteen doors up from the Veysey Store and often referred to as the "working man's store." In 1901, Nettie was also the Assistant Principal for the Hoquiam schools.

JOHN G. CONNELL, a great-grandfather, invented the *Combined Tail Holder and Hopple* in 1900 (Hoquiam):

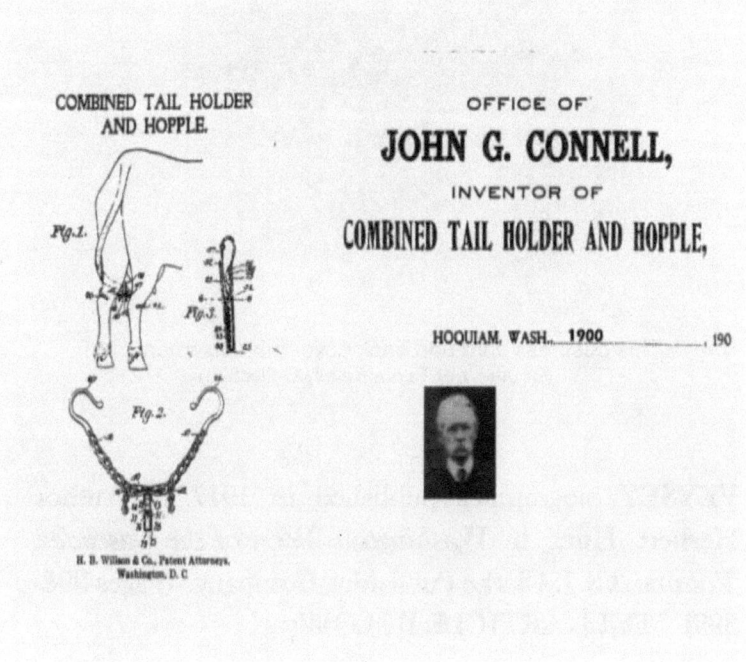

(Courtesy of Taylor Family Collection)

PROFESSOR W.B. WILSON, Magic Healer, also a great-grandfather graduated from the Weltmer Institute, Missouri, and specialized in Magnetic Healing involving telepathy and the suggestion of animals during hypnosis. He first opened his practice in Aberdeen, Washington in 1901. After the Aberdeen fire, he relocated to Hoquiam.

This business card and back cover advertisement card
(Courtesy of Taylor Family Collection)

VEYSEY biographies published in 1917 by Author Herbert Hunt in *Washington, West of the Cascades, Volume 3*, S.J. Clarke Publishing Company. (Pages 398-399) FULL ARTICLE BELOW:

LEON M. VEYSEY, president and manager of the Veysey Brothers Company, general merchants at Montesano, has been identified with the business since 1 1908.[3] He was born on a farm in Waupaca County, Wisconsin, in 1872 and after coming to the west joined his brothers in the conduct of the enterprise of which he is now at the head.

The business was established by Charles and Marion Veysey in 1892 and they opened stores at Montesano, Aberdeen and Hoquiam, later at Elma. The undertaking proved a profitable one from the beginning and in 1905 was incorporated. In that year both of the partners became ill and Marion Veysey passed away, after which the stores at Elma and Hoquiam[4] were closed out and later Charles retired. He and his family, consisting of five children, are now living at Eagle Rock, Los Angeles, California, and he is a very successful real estate dealer and businessman there.

He established the mercantile business in Washington on a small scale, at first handling sewing machines and afterward adding a stock of groceries, making his deliveries with a wheelbarrow. After a little time he was joined by his brother Marion, who, however, returned to California, where he was employed as a streetcar conductor. However, he again came to Washington and

---

[3] Leon arrived in 1902 and managed the Hoquiam store. In 1908, he bought into the business, became president, and relocated to Montesano.
[4] Elma and Hoquiam closed in 1907.

the two brothers were active in the development of the business at Montesano and also conducted a store at Aberdeen.

Through close attention and unfaltering energy, they gained a good start and their business gradually developed, leading to incorporation in 1905, as previously stated.

It was in 1908 that Leon M. Veysey bought into the business, of which he is now president and manager, his attention being given to administrative direction and executive control. He has a well-appointed general merchandise establishment, in which he carries a large stock and the patronage accorded him is gratifying.

CHARLES FRANCES VEYSEY, who throughout the period of an active business life has devoted his attention to law practice, to real estate dealings and to merchandising, is widely known in Montesano and throughout that section of the state. He is now residing at Eagle Rock, and is a very successful real estate dealer and businessman there. He was born at Waupaca, Wisconsin, September 14 1860, a son of Thomas F. and Harriet J. Veysey. The name was originally spelled Vesci or Vescey and the family is descended from Charles Duke of Ingelheim, the son of Charles the Great, King of France. Sire Robert De Vescey accompanied William the Conqueror to England and was given by William the Conqueror a large barony in Lincoln, Northants,

Warwick and Leicester. In 1807 Thomas Veysey, thirty years of age, went to Lexington, Kentucky, where the family lived for two generations, moving to Wisconsin and later to Washington. Charles Frances, Marion E., now deceased, Wallace G., Leon M. and Hattie, representing the third generation in this country, were all born in Waupaca, Wisconsin.

Preparing for the bar, Charles F. Veysey was graduated on the 31st of May, 1883, at Valparaiso, Indiana, with the degree of Bachelor of Laws. His identification with the northwest began in 1886, when he entered the real estate business, and in 1892, he began merchandising in Montesano, Washington, on a small scale, at first handling sewing machines, while afterward he added a stock of groceries to his store, making his deliveries with a wheelbarrow.

A little later, his brother Marion, returning from San Francisco again, joined Charles at Montesano. Charles having at this time stores at Montesano, Aberdeen and Hoquiam, while later a store was also opened at Elma by the brothers. They prospered in the new under-taking from the beginning and in 1905 incorporated the Montesano business. In that year, both of the partners became ill and Marion Veysey died. In 1908 another brother Leon M. Veysey, bought into the business, of which he is now president and manager and later Charles F. Veysey retired.

His brother, however, gives to him the credit for establishing the business and placing it upon its present substantial basis. On the 15th of July, 1903, in Tacoma, Washington, Mr. Veysey was married to Miss Nettie B. Shelley, a daughter of R.L. Shelley, and their children are Neva, Ethel, Inez,[5] Belle, Victor Vincent, and Francis.

The important part which Charles Veysey played in the commercial up-building of various cities of Western Washington and the high regard in which he was uniformly held by his associates and admirers well entitles him to representation in this volume.

---

[5] Charles and first wife Laura had three daughters Neva, Ethel, and Inez.

ACKNOWLEDGMENTS

Thank you to my sister Diane for her collaboration in the writing of this book. Her historical research on our Veysey family, story outlines, and editing have brought this book to life. It would never have happened without her.

Thank you to my husband for all that you do.

Thank you to my Aunt Ruth, always with an encouraging word, and for her proofreading, which aided in this publication.

Thank you to my cousin Vickie for all of her detailed critiques. A tremendous help and much appreciated.

ABOUT THE AUTHOR

KB Taylor's Grays Harbor family history spans back to the 1860s. The author worked as a project-control manager for an aerospace contractor in San Diego and now resides with her husband in Washington State. She is an award winning author whose previous novel is the WILLA Award winner *The Seagirls of the Irene.*

www.ingramcontent.com/pod-product-compliance
Lightning Source LLC
Chambersburg PA
CBHW060352080526
44583CB00012B/272